In the name of God, the Most Gracious,

the Most Merciful.

The World in the Light of a New Perspective on the Use of Technology, Computers and Artificial Intelligence

Written and compiled by:
Parmida Azad

Winter 2024

Dedicated to:

My dear parents, under whose support and harmony I have achieved this goal.

Acknowledgments,

Infinite thanks to the One and Only God,
who granted us existence and guided us
through the path of knowledge and
science,
honoring us with the company of fellow
seekers of wisdom, and blessing us with
the harvest of knowledge and insight.
Also,
endless gratitude to my dear sister, whose
constant support, companionship, and
solidarity have always accompanied me.

Cataloging-in-Publication Data

Author: Azad, Parmida, 2008–
Title: ***The World Through a New Perspective on the Use of Computer Technology and Artificial Intelligence***
/ Compiled and Authored by Parmida Azad.
Publisher: Spot Publisher LLC, Indiana, USA
Description: 186 pages; illustrated (some color), includes color charts.
ISBN: 978-1-962443-16-6
Price: 29 USD
Bibliographic Status: CIP (Cataloging in Publication)
Subject Heading: Artificial intelligence

The World Through a New Perspective on the Use of Computer Technology and Artificial Intelligence

Author and Compiler: Parmida Azad
Layout Designer: Salehiyan Publishing
Publisher: Spot Publisher LLC
Cover Designer: Spot Publisher LLC
Edition and Publication Year: First Edition – 2025
ISBN: 978-1-962443-16-6

Publisher's Office:
5534 Saint Joe Road, Fort Wayne, IN46835,
United States
Tel: +1 (765) 231-6588
Websites: www.spotpub.com

Instagram: @Spotpub2005

Amazon KDP

Table of contents

Chapter 1:

An Overview of the Concept of Artificial Intelligence

Introduction

Artificial Intelligence (AI) is one of the technologies that has garnered considerable attention in recent years. Despite its relatively short lifespan, AI has revolutionized numerous domains and significantly accelerated the pace of progress in many fields. However, as a still-emerging and not yet fully understood technology, its adoption also raises certain concerns. Addressing both the opportunities and challenges associated with AI advancement allows us to leverage its benefits effectively while also managing its risks appropriately. In the following sections, we will discuss these opportunities and challenges to enhance our understanding of AI's broader implications.

The History of Artificial Intelligence: From Origins to Present

Where does the history of AI begin? Which country pioneered the development of artificial intelligence? These are questions most of us have pondered at least once. Today, AI has become one of the most prominent topics in the field of technology. While it may seem that AI has only emerged in the past few years, its roots trace back to the early 1900s. The most significant progress, however, took place in the 1950s, building on the foundational work of early pioneers across various disciplines. Understanding the historical background of AI is essential to comprehending its current state and anticipating its future direction. In this study, we will review major milestones in AI development, from the foundational ideas of the early 20th century to the substantial breakthroughs of recent decades.

What Is Artificial Intelligence?

Artificial Intelligence refers to the development of computers, computer-controlled robots, or software that are capable of performing tasks typically requiring human intelligence. AI systems are designed by analyzing patterns in human cognition and modeling these cognitive processes to create intelligent software and machines. Sometimes referred to as machine intelligence, AI represents the capacity of machines to exhibit intelligent behavior under various conditions—standing in contrast to natural human intelligence.

In other words, AI refers to systems capable of performing actions that resemble human cognitive behaviors, including understanding complex environments, mimicking reasoning processes, responding effectively to challenges, learning, acquiring knowledge, and problem-solving. In most scholarly definitions, AI is characterized as the **science of recognizing and designing intelligent agents**.

AI is a subfield of computer science whose main objective is to create intelligent machines capable of performing tasks that typically require human intelligence. It essentially involves the simulation of human cognition in computers, aiming to design machines that can think, reason, and behave like humans. This concept applies to any machine that can emulate the human mind, particularly in problem-solving and learning. The fundamental goal of AI is built upon three pillars: **learning, reasoning, and perception**.

Narrow Artificial Intelligence

Historically, **Narrow AI** (also known as Weak AI) emerged much earlier than other types of artificial intelligence. Today, there are numerous examples of Narrow AI in action. For instance, AI systems outperform humans in complex tasks such as playing chess, making data-driven business decisions, or completing highly specific assignments.

Narrow AI refers to intelligent systems designed to perform a specific task more efficiently than humans. For example, speech-to-text applications and facial recognition systems that can identify individuals even in crowded spaces are clear illustrations of Narrow AI.

Notable applications of Narrow AI include:

- Self-driving cars that learn to navigate and drive using AI algorithms.
- Image processing and facial recognition systems capable of identifying individuals for security and authentication.
- AI systems that assist with financial transactions in banks and other financial institutions.
- Smart assistants that respond to user needs, book flights, or reserve hotel rooms on behalf of users.

General Artificial Intelligence

General Artificial Intelligence (GAI) refers to a hypothetical machine that could perceive and understand the world as a human does and possess the same cognitive capabilities required for performing everyday tasks. Although AGI does not currently exist, its conceptual form is often found in science fiction.

In theory, a general AI system would possess the ability to reason, solve problems, comprehend language, and adapt to new situations with the flexibility and depth of human cognition. This level of intelligence would require machines to have consciousness, self-awareness, and the capacity to perform any intellectual task that a human can.

Artificial General Intelligence (AGI)

Artificial General Intelligence refers to machines that can operate at the same level as humans or even outperform them in certain areas such as memory and information processing. With this level of awareness and knowledge, a machine can perform all the tasks previously assigned to humans without the need for human involvement. Over time, AGI systems will increasingly be able to replace humans in various fields. Eliminating the need for human presence in many jobs and using AGI technology, like any other technology, can have both positive and negative impacts on human social and individual life. However, despite these concerns, its existence will be highly beneficial and, at the same time, inevitable.

With its vast capabilities and potential to assist humanity, AGI can help solve many of today's global challenges, such as severe climate change. These systems can handle tasks ranging from routine work to highly sensitive and critical operations. At a general level, they may be capable of activities like driving, serving as intelligent personal assistants who understand all user needs, acting as medical assistants or diagnostic systems, and more. At higher levels, AGI systems could be entrusted with tasks that involve human lives, safety, and security—and they would be capable of handling them effectively.

Superintelligence

Superintelligence refers to a type of artificial intelligence that surpasses human-level intelligence and cognition, essentially becoming superhuman. No society has yet achieved this level of AI. In fact, whether we will ever reach superintelligence—and when—is still uncertain. Furthermore, the question of what such an intelligence could do and whether it will be a threat or an opportunity for humanity remains ambiguous. Experts hold very different opinions on this matter, making it a hot topic among tech giants.

To reach the level of superintelligence, an intelligent system must pass the Turing Test. So far, no machine has reached the level of understanding, awareness, and knowledge of a fully grown human to successfully pass this test.

Applications of Artificial Intelligence in Management

The use of AI in management is rapidly expanding as one of its most important applications. AI can be applied to various management processes, including human resource management, financial management, supply chain management, project management, and more.

Using AI algorithms and machine learning, different processes can be managed automatically and accurately. For example, in HR management, AI can automatically screen resumes and identify the best candidates for interviews and hiring. Additionally, AI can manage financial processes and, by analyzing financial data, provide accurate predictions about a company's financial status. It can also be applied in supply chain and project management to improve quality and reduce costs, while enhancing time and cost management.

Other uses of AI in management include enhancing strategic decision-making, predicting customer behavior, and improving user experience. Overall, AI in management leads to increased efficiency and improved company performance.

Applications of Artificial Intelligence in Accounting

AI can be a valuable tool in the field of accounting, helping companies accurately manage financial data and assess financial risks. Some of the specific applications of AI in accounting include:

1. **Financial Data Analysis**: AI can analyze financial data using automated algorithms and machine learning, providing precise predictions about the company's financial outlook.

2. **Fraud Detection**: By analyzing financial patterns, AI can help companies detect

accounting fraud and identify unusual or suspicious transactions.
3. **Risk Forecasting**: AI can assist in predicting financial risks, such as debt risks, price fluctuations, and other market-related concerns.
4. **Financial Management Improvement**: Through automation, AI can help improve financial processes and reduce costs.
5. **Enhancing User Experience**: By analyzing customer data, AI can help improve user experience and provide better services.

Overall, AI helps businesses enhance performance and reduce financial costs, making it a crucial tool in accounting.

Applications of Artificial Intelligence in Economics

AI is considered a critical and vital technology for promoting economic development. Its applications in the field of economics include:

1. **Market Behavior Prediction**: AI can analyze market data, including stock, currency, goods, and services, to predict changes and trends. This helps investors and managers in their decision-making.

2. **Risk Management Improvement**: AI helps companies forecast market changes and enhance their risk management.
3. **Financial Process Optimization**: Automated algorithms can improve financial operations and reduce costs.
4. **Customer Experience Enhancement**: AI can offer better services by analyzing customer financial data.
5. **Financial Forecasting**: AI helps in predicting investment returns and financial performance.
6. **Supply Chain Optimization**: AI can improve supply chain sustainability, reduce costs, and enhance product quality.

AI can also be used in economic and business research, helping to solve complex economic problems and create new research methods. Overall, AI is a powerful tool for improving national and corporate economic performance.

Applications of Artificial Intelligence in Medicine

AI is a modern and essential technology used to enhance healthcare quality and effectiveness. Its applications in medicine include:

1. **Disease Diagnosis**: AI can accurately diagnose diseases by analyzing medical data using automated algorithms. It is used in diagnosing cancer, cardiovascular diseases, neurological disorders, and more.

2. **Disease Prediction**: AI can forecast the likelihood of future illnesses by analyzing patient history and health data, aiding in prevention and early intervention.

3. **Medical Image Analysis**: AI can analyze medical images to detect diseases such as cancer, heart conditions, and neurological issues.

4. **Treatment Process Optimization**: AI can assist doctors in selecting the best treatment methods by analyzing patient data.

5. **Treatment Outcome Prediction**: AI helps in predicting treatment success by analyzing medical history and patient response.

6. **Improvement of E-health Systems**: AI enhances electronic health systems, service quality, and patient experience.

AI also plays a key role in medical research and the development of new drugs, offering innovative ways to address complex healthcare challenges.

Machine Learning Education

Artificial intelligence is based on the concept that human thought processes can be replicated and mechanized. Now it's time to explore the historical background of AI.

A Closer Look at the History of Artificial Intelligence

The roots of artificial intelligence go back thousands of years. In ancient times, inventors created devices called automatons that were mechanical and operated independently of human control. The word *automaton* comes from ancient Greek, meaning "acting on its own." One of the oldest known examples is a mechanical pigeon built around 400 BC by a friend of Plato.

Another famous automaton was designed by Leonardo da Vinci around 1495.

Thanks to early thinkers, AI became more tangible during the 1700s and beyond. Philosophers wondered

how human thought could be artificially replicated by non-human intelligent machines. This curiosity led to the invention of the programmable digital computer known as the Atanasoff–Berry Computer (ABC) in the 1940s.
This invention inspired scientists to pursue the idea of creating an electronic brain or an intelligent artificial being.

Almost a decade later, symbolic reasoning helped shape the conceptual foundations of AI. Alan Turing, a brilliant British mathematician, proposed a test to measure a machine's ability to mimic human behavior so well that it becomes indistinguishable from a real person.

In the late 1950s, during a summer conference at Dartmouth College, computer scientist John McCarthy coined the term *Artificial Intelligence*. He is often considered one of the founding figures in the history of AI.

From the 1950s onward, many scientists, programmers, logicians, and theorists contributed to the modern understanding of AI. Over time, as each decade passed, new innovations emerged that transformed AI from a fantastical concept into a tangible reality for current and future generations.

Early AI Thinking: 1900–1950

In the early 20th century, a wave of new ideas emerged around the concept of artificial humans. Scientists began to ask whether a "mechanical brain" could be created. Some inventors even built early versions of what we now call robots. Although most were relatively simple, they could walk or change facial expressions.

Key milestones from this era include:

- **1921**: Czech playwright Karel Čapek published the science fiction play *R.U.R. (Rossum's Universal Robots)*, where he introduced the term *robot* for the first time.

Year 1929: Makoto Nishimura, a Japanese professor, built the first robot named Dakutens. **Year 1949:** Edmund Callis Berkeley, a computer scientist, published the book *Giant Brains, or Machines That Think*, comparing computer models to the human brain.

If you are interested in learning more about the history of artificial intelligence, where it was created, and who invented it, stay with us in the following article.

The Birth of Artificial Intelligence: 1950–1956

During this period, interest in AI reached its peak. Alan Turing published his research titled *Computing Machinery and Intelligence*, which later became the Turing Test—a standard used to assess computer intelligence. The term "Artificial Intelligencc" was coined and started gaining recognition in academic circles.

Key milestones during this period include:

- **1950:** Alan Turing published *Computing Machinery and Intelligence*, proposing the "Imitation Game" as a test for machine intelligence.
- **1952:** Computer scientist Arthur Samuel developed a program to play the game of Checkers, which was the first program through which a computer could independently learn the game.
- **1955:** John McCarthy, known as the father of AI, held a workshop at Dartmouth on Artificial Intelligence, where the term AI was officially introduced.

Maturation of AI: 1957–1979

From the late 1950s to the 1960s, AI was being developed rapidly. Programming languages still used today were born, and books and movies started exploring robotic concepts.

AI Education

The 1970s witnessed significant advancements such as the creation of the first humanoid robot in Japan and the first automated vehicle built by a graduate student. However, these years also brought struggles, as some governments, including the U.S., lost interest in funding AI research. Key milestones in this period:

- **1958:** John McCarthy invented LISP (List Processing), the first AI programming language still in use today.
- **1961:** Arthur Samuel coined the term "machine learning" for training machines to play chess.
- **1961:** The first industrial robot, Unimate, started work at a General Motors assembly line in New Jersey, handling dangerous tasks like welding.
- **1965:** Edward Feigenbaum and Joshua Lederberg created the first "expert system," an AI programmed to replicate expert decision-making.

- **1966:** Joseph Weizenbaum created the first chatbot, later known as ELIZA.
- **1968:** Soviet mathematician Alexey Ivakhnenko published the "Group Method of Data Handling" in *Avtomatika*, laying the groundwork for what is now known as deep learning.
- **1973:** Mathematician James Lighthill submitted a report to the UK Science Council, criticizing AI's slow progress, leading to reduced government funding.

1979: The American Association for Artificial Intelligence (AAAI) was established.

AI Boom: 1980–1987

The 1980s marked a period of rapid AI growth, known as the "AI Boom." Increased government funding fueled research in deep learning and expert systems. Key milestones:

- **1980:** The first AAAI conference was held at Stanford, and the XCON expert system was commercialized to help configure computer systems based on customer needs.
- **1981:** The Japanese government allocated $850 million to a Fifth Generation Computer Systems

project aiming for human-like reasoning, translation, and speech.

- **1984:** AAAI warned of an impending "AI Winter" due to declining interest and funding.
- **1986:** Ernst Dickmanns and his team at Bundeswehr University in Munich built and demonstrated the first autonomous vehicle, capable of driving at 55 mph.
- **1987:** The first strategic management advisory system, a complex expert system with over 3,000 rules, was launched.

AI Winter: 1987–1993

As predicted by AAAI, the "AI Winter" arrived—a period of declining interest and investment. Both private investors and governments withdrew funding due to high costs and low returns. Key milestones:

- **1987:** The market for LISP-based specialized hardware collapsed due to more affordable alternatives from IBM and Apple. Many LISP-based companies went bankrupt.

- **1988:** Programmer Rollo Carpenter created a chatbot designed for entertaining conversations with humans.

AI Renaissance: 1993–2011

Despite reduced funding, the early 1990s saw major breakthroughs. A notable example is the first AI system to defeat a professional chess player. This era brought innovations like the Roomba smart vacuum and commercial speech recognition software. Increased interest led to renewed funding and progress.

Key milestones:

- **1997:** IBM's Deep Blue defeated world chess champion Garry Kasparov—the first time an AI beat a human champion.
- **1997:** Windows released a speech recognition program developed by Dragon Systems.
- **2000:** Professor Cynthia from Brazil created the first robot capable of simulating human emotions via facial expressions; it was named Kismet.
- **2002:** The first smart vacuum cleaner, Roomba, was released.

- **2003:** Mars rovers "Opportunity" and "Curiosity" landed and moved autonomously on Mars.
- **2006:** Companies like Twitter, Facebook, and Netflix began using AI in advertising algorithms and user experience optimization.
- **2010:** Microsoft launched Xbox 360 Kinect, the first motion-sensing game hardware to translate body movement into gameplay.
- **2011:** IBM's NLP-based computer, Watson, defeated two previous champions on a quiz show.
- **2011:** Apple unveiled Siri, the first popular virtual assistant.

Artificial General Intelligence: 2012–Present

AI tools like virtual assistants and search engines are now widespread.

Key milestones:

- **2012:** Jeff Dean and Andrew Ng from Google designed a neural network capable of identifying cats in unlabeled images.

- **2015:** Elon Musk, Stephen Hawking, Steve Wozniak, and over 3,000 others signed an open letter urging a ban on autonomous weapons.
- **2016:** Hanson Robotics created a humanoid robot named Sophia, who became the first robot to receive citizenship.
- **2017:** Facebook trained two AI chatbots to negotiate, but had to shut them down due to their odd language.
- **2018:** Alibaba's AI outperformed humans in Stanford's reading comprehension test.
- **2019:** Google's AlphaStar AI beat professional players at *StarCraft II*.
- **2020:** OpenAI launched GPT-3 in beta, helping users write code, translate, create content, and answer questions.
- **2021:** OpenAI developed DALL·E, capable of interpreting and generating images with captions—bringing AI closer to visual understanding.
- **2022–2023:** Breakthroughs like ChatGPT, Gemini, and others emerged.

The Future of AI: Outlook and Developments

From humanoid robots like Sophia to smart speakers like Alexa, AI is evolving rapidly. One day, intelligent companions may exist indistinguishably from humans. But when? Possibly sooner than we think.

Definition of AI and Why Its Future Matters

AI involves developing smart machines and systems that mimic human intelligence, including speech recognition, imagination, decision-making, and problem-solving. AI integrates machine learning, language processing, and deep learning. Forecasting AI's future matters because it affects all aspects of life: economy, culture, security. As AI evolves, its decision-making ability raises concerns—such as autonomous cars making life-or-death decisions. Ethical frameworks for AI are essential. AI may also increase unemployment by replacing human jobs or make biased decisions affecting lives. Thus, exploring AI's future—across cultural, political, and social dimensions—is crucial for managing its impact.

Opportunities Ahead for AI

AI holds vast potential to enhance the future. It has already significantly improved many fields. It can automate repetitive tasks, boost productivity, improve healthcare diagnostics and treatment, and assist human decision-making by analyzing huge data sets instantly.

Key Opportunities Include:

Improved Services and Products

AI can analyze large datasets to offer valuable insights to product makers and service providers. For instance, AI can personalize products based on customer preferences and launch targeted advertising campaigns using user feedback.

AI helps companies maintain product quality by identifying real-time issues in production processes.

Increased Productivity and Cost Reduction

AI can streamline workflows, reduce time spent on repetitive tasks, and boost workplace efficiency. For example, it can handle dangerous or monotonous jobs in manufacturing, significantly cutting costs

Artificial intelligence can shorten the trial-and-error process in various innovations by simulating complex scientific scenarios, enabling scientists to search more quickly in their fields of interest. This can also enhance collaboration among scientists and experts across different domains, accelerating progress in new sciences. Experts can review numerous articles and books more rapidly using AI. Previously, scientists had to spend a lot of time studying a specific subject, but with AI, this time can be significantly reduced, increasing work efficiency.

Challenges and Potential Threats Although AI has the potential to revolutionize various industries and can significantly ease human life, it also presents several challenges and threats that must be considered before fully embracing it. Ignoring these issues could lead to harmful impacts on individuals' lives and cause worrying consequences. In the future, AI will present not only opportunities but also challenges and threats that may cause concerns about its performance. For instance, AI requires a large amount of data to function well, and obtaining such data can be difficult in some fields. Additionally, AI algorithms might unintentionally make biased decisions, compromising social justice. Moreover, AI systems operate autonomously in decision-making, raising ethical concerns about the correctness of these decisions.

Some of the most important challenges and threats expected in the future of AI include:

Replacement of Human Workforce and Unemployment One of the main concerns about the future of AI is the increased possibility of unemployment due to technological advancements. Since AI systems are designed to automate many tasks, some industries worry about human workers losing their jobs. For example, automation on production lines can reduce the need for factory workers. Additionally, AI-driven algorithms and programs may decrease the demand for personnel in customer service and management roles. Rising unemployment could cause social problems and reduce job opportunities for humans. Generally, factory workers and those working in company support and sales departments are more likely to be threatened by AI. AI can perform their jobs automatically on production lines with greater speed, accuracy, and much lower cost. Furthermore, AI can provide after-sales services and respond to customer queries instantly and efficiently. Job loss can also negatively affect the mental health of many individuals and make their livelihoods challenging.

This issue is one of the most critical aspects of AI development and expansion that must not be overlooked. However, some believe AI can also create entirely new job opportunities, increasing the demand for skilled and experienced individuals. Despite automation and loss of some jobs, new roles requiring human experience and skills will emerge. Programming robots, training AI, and expertise in data science are examples of opportunities that can arise. Still, adapting the workforce to these new job roles may be challenging and present its own difficulties.

Security and Privacy Risks To be effective, AI needs access to vast amounts of data, and this dependency raises concerns about data security. For example, widespread AI use can increase surveillance, leading to the recording and analysis of individuals' personal behaviors. This may threaten privacy laws and allow government and private companies to misuse personal data for their benefit. Additionally, the security of AI systems themselves is worrisome. As AI becomes more complex and autonomous, malicious actors might exploit system vulnerabilities. This could lead to hacking, intentional data manipulation, and even physical harm to people and property. Therefore, strict regulations, ethical guidelines, and frameworks are crucial in AI's future development. AI has the potential to share sensitive information like location, interests, and personal habits without an individual's consent. This can increase the risk of identity theft and cause significant troubles. Moreover, AI can be used to manipulate data, distribute malware, and conduct cyber-attacks. Thus, careful examination of all aspects and eliminating security weaknesses is necessary before fully trusting this technology.

Lack of Transparency and Accountability AI systems often work like a "black box," making it hard to understand how a specific decision was made. This opacity raises concerns about responsibility and fairness in AI's decisions. For instance, if AI is used in hiring, loan approvals, or criminal justice processes, it's difficult to ensure that its decisions are fair and free from bias. Biases might exist in the algorithms AI uses, leading to harmful effects on individuals' lives. Furthermore, AI systems may avoid taking responsibility for their actions. If an AI makes a significant mistake, it must be held accountable, and those harmed by the error should have recourse. Lack of accountability makes controlling AI systems difficult and can lead to bigger threats. Researchers and developers should prioritize transparency and accountability in AI design and never overlook these issues.

Legal Challenges with AI

Until a decade ago, AI was mostly limited to specialized technical fields understood only by experts. Now, AI is part of everyday life. Self-driving cars are approaching regulatory approval, insurance companies use AI algorithms to analyze customer risk and set premiums, and security software helps law enforcement monitor individuals with criminal records. While AI may simplify many lives, it raises serious legal and judicial questions. For example, many militaries are developing autonomous war robots. Is it ethical to let a computer program control weapon firing? If such a weapon mistakenly destroys a hospital or refugee shelter, who is legally responsible for the casualties? These complex questions highlight the challenges AI poses in legal contexts. AI's decision-making automates many tasks, reducing human involvement. Citizens might initiate processes through tools that automatically analyze their information and deliver results without human contact. While this can streamline governance, it raises concerns about trust and fairness. For instance, China has implemented a massive social credit system collecting data on payments and social relationships to score citizens' creditworthiness. AI software and algorithms continue to evolve, but legal systems struggle to keep up. What happens if AI's decision-making results in harm? How can errors be challenged when AI is a "black box"? There is no clear answer yet, but continuous monitoring and oversight systems may be needed.

AI can reduce corruption by eliminating human discretion and bribery opportunities, ensuring consistent application of laws. However, it may also remove flexibility needed for individualized decisions. Some cases require exceptions—such as emergency vehicles ignoring traffic rules—which rigid algorithms cannot handle.

The scope of AI's authority is also a concern. People accept AI in routine tasks like tax calculations but may resist giving AI control over fundamental rights like life, liberty, or fair trial. There is also fear that AI might influence human judges or policymakers toward unfair decisions. Thus, legal and ethical safeguards are essential.

Conclusion

AI's integration into society offers immense benefits but also poses significant ethical, legal, and social challenges. Addressing these issues thoughtfully is necessary to ensure AI serves humanity fairly, securely, and transparently.

Artificial intelligence has been elevated to a level of superior complexity and application, and today it is recognized as one of the important and vital terms in the world of technology and science.

While artificial intelligence helps human society in various dimensions and has significant positive impacts in fields such as industry, healthcare, transportation, education, and more, these advancements have also created new challenges and questions for jobs and various sectors. Among these, the field of law and advocacy, as one of the vital areas of society related to the protection of rights and interests of individuals and organizations, is also facing potential impacts of artificial intelligence.

In the end, it can be said that the future of artificial intelligence is accompanied by many uncertainties and it is not possible to give a definitive opinion about it. This technology can simultaneously create opportunities and challenges for humans and in some cases be beneficial and in others dangerous. Artificial intelligence can create new opportunities in areas such as healthcare, economy, and transportation, each of which can experience unprecedented progress. This technology can revolutionize any field it enters by improving efficiency, accuracy, and effectiveness of human activities. On the other hand, the advancement of artificial intelligence can be somewhat concerning due to challenges such as increasing unemployment rates among human societies and security disruptions. To ensure the proper and safe functioning of artificial intelligence, it is better to control its operations within the framework of laws and regulations. Investment in educational programs can also better prepare people to face these challenges. In fact, individuals can develop their skills in a way that allows them to adapt to artificial intelligence and use it to their advantage. Foresight regarding artificial intelligence and attention to all aspects of its progress can help ensure its proper use and greatly reduce the likelihood of harm to various pillars of society and individuals.

Chapter 2

Concepts of Artificial Intelligence and How It Is Trained

Introduction

Recent advances in artificial intelligence, especially in the third generation of models like Claude 3.7 and Grok 3, represent a fundamental leap in the capabilities of this technology to process and analyze complex problems. These models, relying on immense computational power and novel scaling methods, have not only increased the speed and accuracy of data understanding and processing but have also enabled researchers to propose and solve more complex challenges. As a result, new horizons in AI research and development have opened. Examining the exceptional capabilities of these new models, including precise coding, advanced data analysis, and multimedia content creation, shows that this technology goes beyond merely automating everyday tasks.

Today, innovative aspects of these models, such as deep reasoning abilities and multi-level coordination in information processing, have paved the way for AI to become a real assistant and partner for professionals in scientific, industrial, and even creative fields.

Enhancing Computational Power and Its Impact on Performance

According to Ethan Mollick's note on the website "One Useful Thing," the growth in computational power for training AI models has created an unprecedented leap in their quality and processing speed. Among these, Grok 3, developed by xAI led by Elon Musk, surpasses GPT-4 thanks to its higher computational capacity, improving the accuracy and richness of outputs in diverse domains. This advancement in learning patterns has not only enhanced logical inference and abstract thinking but also paved the way to solving complex, multifaceted problems. Similarly, Claude 3.7, utilizing comparable computational capacities, has achieved deeper data analysis, formulation of difficult issues, and precise solutions across a broad range of scientific fields. According to "scaling laws," the greater the amount of data and computational power, the more precise responses, complex inferences, and exponential performance improvements models can provide. This process allows AI engineers to scale model capacity according to research or industrial demand and opens paths to discovering new training and optimization methods.

Scaling and New Frontiers of Computational Power

Existing documents indicate that each unit improvement in AI model performance generally requires tenfold increases in computational power. This clearly shows a nonlinear relationship between computational capacity and output quality in these technologies since AI capabilities do not grow linearly with resource consumption but increase exponentially. Under these conditions, large investments in computational infrastructure—including developing specialized data centers and upgrading advanced hardware such as GPUs and tensor processing units—are unavoidable. The goal of these investments is not only to increase processing speed but also to improve stability, reliability, and scalability, enabling models to process vast amounts of data while exhibiting higher inferential power.

At this complexity level, third-generation models now reach up to 2×10^26 FLOPS during training. This staggering figure becomes more tangible when considering it equates to the continuous operation of a smartphone for 634,000 years or the Apollo guidance computer for 79 trillion years. This massive scale not only signals the transition from a conventional era to a new epoch in AI system development but also introduces the novel concept of "hypercomputation." This infrastructural evolution enables AI models to recognize more complex data patterns and respond much faster and more efficiently to multifaceted problems. Consequently, organizations and research centers will need this level of computational power not only to enhance current capabilities but also to create innovative R&D pathways.

Second Scaling Law and Emergence of Reasoning Models

Analysis charts show that dedicating more computational time to a model affects not only its speed but also significantly deepens its reasoning ability. This approach allows models to operate in multi-step, more flexible processes, where each stage receives and analyzes the previous stage's output, allocating more computational resources if needed to reach a more accurate answer. Such architectures form reasoning systems based on dynamic algorithms capable of managing computational resources to solve complex problems.

These systems' role goes beyond simultaneous data processing; relying on principles such as "chain of thought" and iterative optimization, they enable models to apply multi-step question-answering strategies or multi-faceted analyses when facing difficult queries. This capability is clearly demonstrated in the performance of Claude 3.7 by Anthropic. For example, when executing complex coding tasks, this model can repeatedly revise its hypotheses about code structure and implementation, gaining a deeper understanding of related scientific concepts. Practically, such advanced reasoning capacity is a prerequisite for entering advanced research fields in basic sciences and engineering, where the model must process multi-step information and continuously update its predictions or codes.

Practical Applications Across Various Fields

The ability of these models is not merely theoretical; multiple evidences show that third-generation models, especially Claude 3.7 and Grok 3, have succeeded in diverse applications. Claude 3.7, in particular, can interact in natural language, generate executable codes, and create 3D and visual content—abilities widely used in scientific simulations, industrial design, and entertainment. Leveraging high inferential power, this model manages coding processes more creatively and can transform complex instructions into actionable solutions.

On the other hand, Grok 3, with extensive processing power and high research capacity, is ideal for interdisciplinary studies. For example, in big data research projects, this advanced model can detect hidden patterns in massive datasets and present results as structured reports or charts. These capabilities, ranging from coding and data analysis to multimedia content generation, show that third-generation AI models are not only theoretically powerful but have also become serious and efficient tools for advancing research, industry, and creative goals.

Organizational Paradigm Shift: From Automation to Collaboration

While automation remains the priority in many organizations, advanced models like Claude 3.7 and Grok 3 go beyond simplifying processes and pave the way for transforming managerial and research perspectives. These systems, based on three key components—deep analytical ability, computational creativity, and high-speed data processing—can serve as a "cognitive partner" rather than just auxiliary tools alongside specialists.

In fact, working with these models can transform traditional automation into a more dynamic concept based on human-AI collaboration. For example, in academic research, these models analyze vast data volumes and discover hidden patterns while suggesting creative research questions and new potential approaches, opening new horizons for researchers. In big data analytics, rather than merely repeating predefined formulas, these models uncover complex multi-layered patterns to assist managers in strategic decision-making.

Moreover, leveraging the creative computational capacity of third-generation models enables specialists to generate ideas beyond conventional frameworks. In strategic planning, combining up-to-date business data with AI's reasoning and processing capabilities can accelerate decision-making and increase the diversity and depth of proposed options. Experts believe this interactive approach between humans and AI heralds an era where task completion time reduces while quality and innovation reach unprecedented levels.

Ultimately, the emergence of Claude 3.7 and Grok 3 symbolizes an evolutionary phase in AI, built upon immense computational power and precise scaling strategies. These advances facilitate novel scientific and industrial methods and elevate AI's role from mere automation to a creative and collaborative presence. Close cooperation between humans and AI in many fields—from new product development to multidisciplinary research—is taking shape and may transform traditional innovation structures.

At the same time, challenges such as high infrastructure costs, ethical issues related to data privacy, and legal and regulatory complexities remain. Nevertheless, current progress trends indicate these obstacles will eventually be manageable or solvable, thanks to AI's broad benefits. Furthermore, the increasing integration of AI with foundational technologies like the Internet of Things and cognitive sciences opens new prospects in healthcare, education, smart transportation, and even digital art creation.

Therefore, the future outlook points to AI's growing influence in research, industrial activities, and organizational processes. This approach not only reduces time and costs but also leads to innovative solutions previously unimaginable. In such an environment, the paradigm shift from mere automation to comprehensive human-AI collaboration will undoubtedly become the dominant and sustainable mode in future technological ecosystems.

General Definitions of Artificial Intelligence:

Artificial Intelligence

Many people still associate the term "artificial intelligence" with robots and imagine them as emotionless machines designed to simplify tasks and eventually replace humans. This perception is largely influenced by science fiction movies, but reality is quite different. AI, often abbreviated as AI, is actually a technology that possesses a form of thinking ability. Although this thinking differs significantly from human thought, it aims to imitate it.

Today, AI may not exist exactly as imagined in fiction, but many everyday activities—such as internet searching or browsing social media—are influenced by AI, often without us noticing. We have become so accustomed to this usage that we rarely realize when AI is operating in the background. The main reason is a lack of understanding of what AI truly is and what it can do. Since the future belongs to AI, instead of fearing it, we should learn what we can achieve with it and deepen our knowledge in this field. So, let's start from the beginning and understand what AI is.

Definition of AI

There is no universally agreed-upon definition of AI among scientists, but most definitions fall into four categories:

1. Thinks like a human
2. Thinks logically
3. Acts like a human
4. Acts logically

The first two relate to processes of thinking and reasoning, while the latter two focus on behavior.

A Simple Definition of AI

Artificial Intelligence is a branch of computer science whose main goal is to create intelligent machines capable of performing tasks requiring human intelligence. AI essentially simulates human intelligence for computers and refers to machines programmed to think like humans and imitate human behavior. This definition applies to any machine that operates similarly to the human mind and can perform tasks such as problem-solving and learning.

Goals of AI

The foundation of AI is to define human intelligence and its functioning in a way that machines can execute and correctly perform assigned tasks. The objectives of AI rest on three pillars:

1. Machine learning from data and adapting based on experience.
2. Ability to analyze and understand complex concepts and data.
3. Decision-making capability based on available information.

In summary, AI is designed to develop machines that can function independently, learn from experiences, and make decisions to solve problems effectively. Humanity faces many problems that today's humans struggle with, such as severe climate changes, which will be solved.

General artificial intelligence systems can perform tasks ranging from ordinary to very important and critical in the best way. At the general level, they can do tasks like driving, being an intelligent personal assistant capable of understanding all user needs, a medical assistant or a disease diagnosis system, and so on. At higher levels, these systems can perform tasks related to life, security, and human lives and can manage such tasks well.

Super Artificial Intelligence

Super artificial intelligence is a term used for AI that surpasses human intelligence and understanding, essentially possessing superhuman intelligence. So far, no society has achieved super artificial intelligence. In fact, whether or not it will be reached and when it might happen is shrouded in uncertainty. Also, what such AI will do or whether it will be a threat or an opportunity for humanity is unclear, and many experts hold very different opinions, making it a hot debate among technology giants. To reach this level of AI, an intelligent system must pass the Turing test, and no machine has yet reached the level of understanding, consciousness, and breadth of knowledge of an adult human to pass this test successfully.

Difference Between Narrow AI, General AI, and Super AI

Narrow (weak) AI is where we currently are, general AI is the future we aim to reach, and super AI is the future we envision for AI as a result of its evolution and becoming intelligent.

Narrow AI means the system applies a certain level of intelligence in a specific domain. Essentially, this system is still a computer, but one that operates smarter than humans in some fields.

The meaning of general AI is much more complex. This term refers to a system that can perform any task assigned to it like a human. The ideal general AI can have empirical understanding and broad cognition of its environment and can process data and information several times faster than humans. Thus, we can say general AI systems will outperform humans in terms of knowledge, cognitive ability, and processing speed. The important point is that this system is born from human brain and science.

As mentioned, super AI is when AI surpasses human abilities. This system can have powers that humans lack. Achieving this system will result from the evolution of general AI, and it can be created by humans or by intelligent systems that have evolved.

Training Artificial Intelligence

Today, AI systems become intelligent with the help of machine learning and deep learning and can learn and be trained.

Machine Learning

Machine learning is a subset of AI that enables systems to learn and improve automatically without needing specific programming for each learning task. The main focus of machine learning is developing programs that, by accessing data, automatically use it for their own learning.

In machine learning, the learning process starts with observations or data, and the system uses examples, direct experiences, instructions, etc., to find a pattern and based on it begins decision-making and problem-solving. The main goal of machine learning is to allow the computer to learn automatically without human intervention and adjust its behavior based on observations and data. Many different algorithms exist for machine learning, and hundreds of new algorithms are created daily. Typically, these algorithms are grouped by learning style such as supervised learning, unsupervised learning, semi-supervised learning, or by their form and function like classification, regression, decision trees, clustering, deep learning, etc.

Regardless of grouping, all machine learning algorithms generally operate in the following areas:

- Representation: a set of classifiers or language understood by the computer.
- Evaluation: also known as objective function/scoring.
- Optimization: a search method; usually a classifier with the highest score. The fundamental goal of machine learning algorithms is successful interpretation of data and generalizing learnings beyond the training samples.

Deep Learning

Deep learning is a type of machine learning and AI that mimics how the human brain learns a specific topic. This type of learning is an important element in data science, which includes statistics and predictive modeling. Deep learning is highly useful for data scientists who collect, analyze, and interpret large amounts of data, making the analysis and interpretation faster and easier. In a way, deep learning is machine learning applied to complex tasks, representation, or abstraction, allowing AI systems to gain a better understanding of existential realities and identify various patterns. At the simplest level, deep learning can be seen as a way to automate the analysis of predictions.

To understand how deep learning works, you need to be familiar with neural networks. This learning is essentially done through neural networks with many hidden layers, and the deeper you go in these layers, the more complex and complete the models become.

Categories of AI Systems

Arnet Hintz, Assistant Professor of Integrative Biology and Computer Science at Michigan State University, divides AI into four main categories. This classification covers systems that exist today and emotional systems that do not yet exist. These categories are:

Type 1: Reactive Machines

An example is Deep Blue, a chess program that in the 1990s defeated Garry Kasparov, the world chess champion. Deep Blue could recognize pieces on each chess square and predict upcoming moves. The problem was it could not remember past experiences or use them for future moves. This program analyzed all possible strategic moves each time and chose the best. Such AI and similar programs are usable for limited goals and cannot easily be applied in other situations.

Type 2: Limited Memory

Unlike the previous, this AI system can use past experiences for future decisions. Some decision-making features in self-driving cars are designed this way. These machines use observations for decisions they will soon make, like changing lanes. However, these observations and experiences are not stored permanently.

Type 3: Theory of Mind

This type does not yet exist but is based on the psychological concept of understanding beliefs, knowledge, desires, intentions of individuals, and how these affect decisions. This AI would be capable of understanding and analyzing such decision-making.

Type 4: Self-awareness

In this category, AI systems possess self-awareness and consciousness. Such machines understand their state and can infer others' emotions based on the information they gather. This type, like Type 3, does not yet exist.

Is Robotics the Same as Artificial Intelligence?

Robotics is a field of science and technology dealing with robots. Generally, robots are machines programmed to perform certain tasks automatically or semi-automatically. Robotics involves design, construction, and programming of robots, and only a small part of it relates to AI, which merges with robotics to form intelligent robots. AI is a subset of computer science that produces programs to perform tasks requiring human intelligence. AI algorithms involve learning, understanding, problem-solving, natural language processing, or logical reasoning. AI has diverse and widespread applications worldwide, used to automate or smarten processes in various fields. For example, Google's search engine uses AI to find the best and closest results to what the user wants. AI algorithms are not designed solely for robot control. When AI is used for robot control, it is only part of a larger robotic system that includes sensors, actuators, and programming where AI may not be involved. AI and robotics are completely separate sciences with no similarity except that AI is used in some parts to make robots intelligent.

Applications of AI in Various Businesses

AI can be used in many businesses and brings many benefits.

AI in Healthcare

The most important point is improving patient outcomes while reducing costs. Healthcare companies want to use machine learning to improve and speed diagnosis and treatment. One well-known technology in this field is a system that understands natural language and can answer questions posed to it. This system extracts all patient information from available sources to generate a hypothesis and presents it after confirmation. Other AI programs like chatbots help patients schedule appointments, answer questions, issue bills, or act as virtual health assistants giving medical feedback.

AI in Business

For repetitive tasks done by humans in any business, robotic process automation can be used. Machine learning algorithms can integrate with analytics and CRM to better serve customers by discovering needed information. Chatbots can also provide instant customer service on websites.

AI in Education

AI can help automate grading and student ranking, giving teachers more time. It can assess students and adapt to their needs, working with each individual at their pace. AI tutoring systems can provide more support and ensure students' learning is on track. AI can change how and where students learn and even replace some teachers.

AI in Economy

AI systems in personal finance apps like Mint or Turbo Tax collect individual financial data and offer financial advice. Other programs like IBM Watson can assist in home buying. Today, software handles a large part of Wall Street trading.

AI in Law and Judiciary

Finding documents and evidence is often difficult for humans. Automation and AI can help this process and make it more efficient. Startups are building computer assistants that filter questions and answers and can review, classify, and respond to programmed ontological queries.

AI in Manufacturing

Robots can fully perform assigned tasks, operating independently of human workers.

AI in Security

AI and image processing tech are used in security for tracking criminals, identifying offenders, etc. These systems can recognize faces, objects, and detect violations or criminal acts, alerting relevant authorities.

AI and Data Interpretation

Big data refers to large amounts of structured and unstructured data. Big data can be used to extract needed information for important decisions and execute strategic moves with greater accuracy. A data scientist can analyze not only people's needs but also market laws and trends using big data. Analyzing such large amounts of data is impossible without intelligent systems because of the volume and increasing rate of data. Thus, using AI in big data interpretation leads to many new concepts that can transform large parts of society and human life.

Challenges of AI

The application of AI is not without challenges and risks. Ethical issues, data privacy, transparency, bias in training data, and job displacement due to automation are significant concerns. Many researchers and policymakers are actively working to develop guidelines and regulations to manage these risks.

The ability of machines to learn on their own—without waiting for pre-written human input—marked a major shift. This delegation of the learning process from humans to machines accelerated the development of machine learning, enabling the creation of AI programs that could truly learn from experience.

Modern Artificial Intelligence

Major advances followed soon after. In the first decade of the 21st century, progress in object recognition allowed developers to create powerful AI capable of accurately identifying objects based on a set of images—without the need for manual coding or decoding.

The same machine learning approach was used in the advanced AI that discovered the antibiotic *Halicin*. Researchers at MIT developed a sophisticated machine learning algorithm that could *predict* the antibacterial properties of molecules. They trained it using a dataset of 2,000 different molecules. The result was something beyond the reach of any human expert or traditional algorithm.

In this case, the machine learning algorithm developed a new model based on the available data and was able to detect and understand patterns that were previously hidden from human perception and not bound by any predefined rules. As mentioned earlier, this form of modern AI doesn't require human-defined cause-and-effect relationships to learn. For example, modern AI can identify the most promising job applicants among a large pool and, based on real-world feedback, predict outcomes and analyze uncertainties effectively. In essence, machine learning algorithms follow a sequence of steps similar to classical algorithms, but rather than directly arriving at fixed outcomes, they assess the quality of potential results to enable meaningful learning. Generally, the more data neural networks receive and the more layers they have, the better they can identify underlying relationships. That's why today's deep learning systems use multi-layered neural networks—sometimes up to ten layers. However, it's important to note that neural networks are highly resource-intensive. Their processes demand significant computational power and complex algorithms capable of analyzing and adapting massive datasets.

In reality, AI doesn't learn like humans and then apply what it has learned. Instead, it focuses its efforts on two distinct phases: **training** and **inference**. During the training phase, evaluation and optimization algorithms are used to assess and improve the AI's performance to achieve desirable outcomes. In the case of *Halicin*, this involved identifying relationships between molecular structures and the antibiotic's effectiveness based on the training data.

In the inference phase, researchers tasked the AI with identifying potential new antibiotics.

Chapter 3
Artificial Intelligence Learning

Introduction

Artificial Intelligence (AI) involves creating computer programs capable of simulating tasks related to human intelligence. This field of technology tackles challenges using computer programming and large datasets. Within the realm of AI are machine learning, deep learning, and natural language processing, which enable computers to acquire knowledge through experience and perform tasks similar to human abilities, often surpassing human efficiency.

Stages of Artificial Intelligence Learning

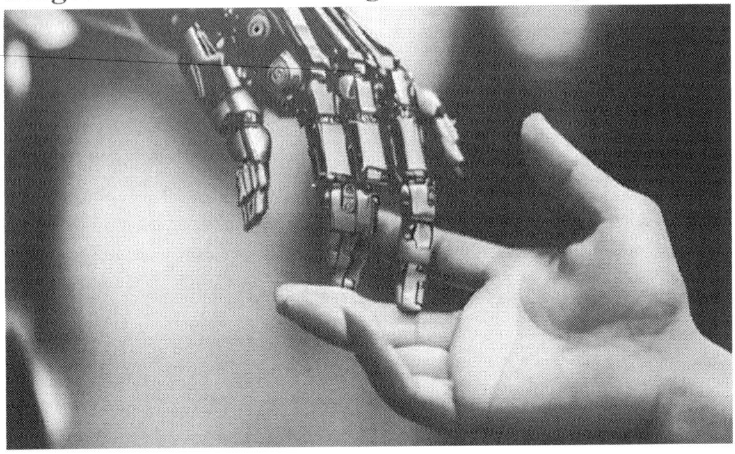

Artificial Intelligence (AI) is a new and constantly expanding field. However, we have not yet reached the vision of intelligent robots depicted in science fiction movies, but today AI is seamlessly intertwined in our daily lives.

Why Learn Artificial Intelligence?

Learning AI is important for the following reasons:

1. **Ability to Solve Complex Problems:** AI can automatically and quickly solve complex problems that humans cannot.
2. **Improving Efficiency:** AI can enhance workflows and increase efficiency by automating repetitive and time-consuming processes optimally.
3. **Prevention and Prediction:** AI can analyze big data to identify hidden patterns and trends, providing accurate predictions about future events. This capability is useful in many fields such as weather forecasting, risk management, disease prevention, and more.
4. **Creating New Possibilities:** AI can be used to develop new capabilities and services like smart cars, intelligent home robots, and more.

5. **Enhancing Security:** AI helps identify and track threats and vulnerabilities in systems, thereby improving security.
6. **Facilitating Decision Making:** By analyzing data and providing precise information to decision-makers, AI simplifies the decision-making process.
7. **Ability to Learn and Update:** AI can improve itself using learning algorithms and perform better with experience. In other words, AI continuously learns and demonstrates superiority over previous systems.

What is Artificial Intelligence?

Artificial Intelligence (AI) involves creating computer programs capable of simulating tasks related to human intelligence. This technology uses computer programming and large datasets to address challenges. The realm of AI includes machine learning, deep learning, and natural language processing, which enable computers to acquire knowledge through experience and perform tasks similar to human abilities, often surpassing human efficiency.

This type of AI is known as narrow or weak AI, which we discussed in detail in the section on types of artificial intelligence. In these cases, computers excel in specific tasks by recognizing patterns in vast datasets.

Another type is limited AI, which, although adaptable based on inputs, is restricted to predefined parameters. Nonetheless, its applications remain significant. The advent of the Fourth Industrial Revolution and early digital ethics in modern businesses generates massive amounts of data, which serve as fuel for applications driven by narrow AI. On the other side, there is strong AI. Strong AI, also known as Artificial General Intelligence (AGI), represents the type of AI often portrayed in science fiction. The realization of such AI is not imminent, even though developers have persistently tackled AGI-related challenges and produced new models. The following provides explanations about learning artificial intelligence from scratch.

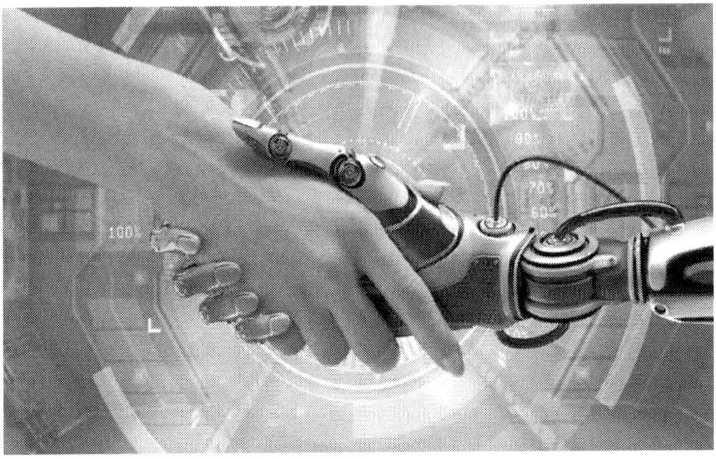

What Does an Artificial Intelligence Engineer Do?
The tasks and responsibilities of an AI engineer may vary depending on the specific field they work in. Generally, AI engineers are engaged in building AI systems and applications aimed at improving decision-making processes and refining performance metrics.

The role of an AI engineer is multifaceted and complex, requiring skills in the following areas:

- Achieving goals through skilled use of AI models.
- Innovating solutions by combining logical reasoning, probabilistic analysis, and machine learning techniques.

- Monitoring and guiding development initiatives by thoroughly analyzing complex systems.
- Gaining deep understanding and effectively implementing best practices related to speech recognition, data processing, data mining, and robotics.

What Are the Steps to Learn Artificial Intelligence?

You might ask yourself: How do I start learning AI? Where do I begin? Learning AI from scratch requires going through several stages. Below are 8 summarized steps to start learning AI:

1. Learn prerequisites and fundamental principles of AI
2. Learn theoretical concepts of AI
3. Develop data processing skills
4. Create and participate in AI projects
5. Get familiar with AI tools
6. Enroll in AI-related courses
7. Do internships in the AI field
8. Get hired and start working in AI

Starting AI from scratch has its own challenges that anyone aiming to learn it must confront. Also, learning advanced mathematics and logic related to AI concepts can ease the path into this field. Below, we explore the AI learning roadmap more deeply through these 8 stages.

Prerequisites for Learning AI from Scratch
Before starting to learn AI from zero, you need a strong foundation in the following areas:

- Statistics and probability
- Mathematics
- Programming skills
- Data structures
- Algorithmic principles

Basics of Probability and Statistics
Probability and statistics form a fundamental pillar in AI, serving as a basis for teaching computers to handle uncertainty. AI learning systems operate through understanding data, which underpins statistical insights. Probability and statistics help answer questions such as:

- What is the most likely outcome?
- What predictions can be made about outcomes?
- What are the patterns in the data?

The domain of probability and statistics in AI covers key topics like:

- Functions that define probability distributions
- Population parameter estimation
- Hypothesis testing
- Numerical and visual data representation
- Key aspects of probability theory
- Distribution of sampled data

Mathematical Foundations for AI

To complement your skills in probability and statistics, understanding core mathematical concepts is essential to learn AI from scratch. This includes:

- Learning coordinate systems and nonlinear transformations, which are integral to AI
- Mastering linear and higher-order regression to facilitate predictive insights from datasets
- Learning logistic regression for data classification
- Numerical analysis to convert mathematical formulas into efficient code implementations
- Linear algebra as the cornerstone for understanding AI and machine learning methods
- Basic knowledge of differential calculus and specific aspects of multivariable calculus, crucial

for handling parameter changes, functions, errors, and approximations

Programming Skills

Gaining proficiency in AI programming languages is vital for building AI applications. Notable options include:

- Lisp, the second oldest programming language used in AI
- SQL, primarily used in database management
- Python, popular for its accessibility, simplicity, abundant libraries, and extensive educational resources
- Java, valued for user-friendliness and cross-platform compatibility
- R, designed for managing large datasets

Data Structures for Learning AI from Scratch

In AI, data serves as the essential input. Data structures encompass various techniques for systematically organizing data to maximize utility. For those eager to learn AI from scratch, mastering the selection and application of optimal data structures for specific programs is very important.

A thorough understanding of these structures enables AI enthusiasts to effectively manage data and enhances their ability to develop impactful and efficient AI applications.

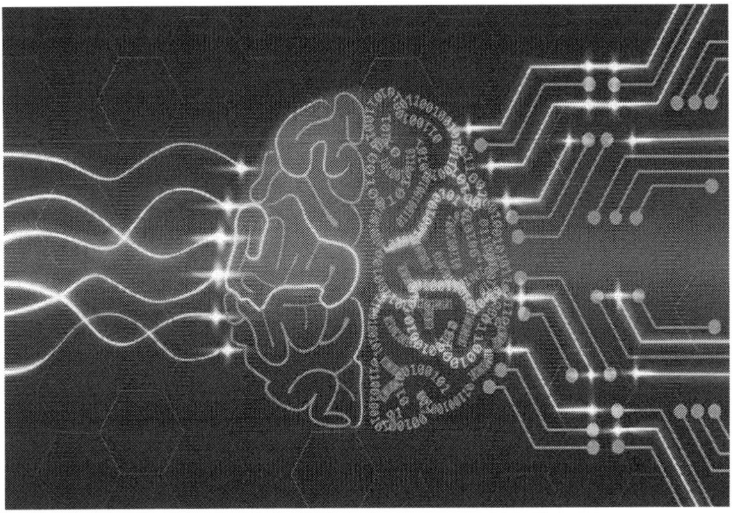

Mastering AI Theory

After acquiring the essential prerequisites for learning AI from scratch, the next step is diving into AI theory. Regardless of the path you choose—be it in-person classes, online courses, or self-study—you must become familiar with the theoretical principles of artificial intelligence. Below are some core concepts that form the foundation of AI education:

Developing Problem-Solving Skills

The essence of AI lies in its ability to tackle complex challenges. This requires the skillful deployment of a variety of techniques, including algorithms and heuristics. At the core of an AI system is an agent operating within a dynamic environment. In AI, the agent represents a program that guides the decision-making process. In this context, a problem-solving agent focuses solely on achieving its goal through reasoning. To pave the way for solving problems, a process of problem formulation emerges, which involves key elements such as:

1. The cost associated with each path taken
2. The initial state of the agent's environment
3. A transition model detailing the effects of actions
4. Goal testing to determine if the objective has been met
5. The set of possible actions available to the agent

Mastering these principles enables you to fully understand the complexities of problem-solving in AI—a cornerstone of your journey toward AI proficiency.

Understanding Natural Language

Natural Language Understanding (NLU) is a specialized area of AI that uses programming techniques to decode human speech. It enables computers to understand human communication without the rigid syntax of programming languages. NLU facilitates two-way interaction between humans and machines. In this realm, AI algorithms are employed to interpret human speech and convert it into structured data. This includes sentiment analysis, named entity recognition, and identification of numerical entities.

Data Transformation

Learning AI from scratch requires a deep understanding of data manipulation. Since AI relies heavily on datasets for learning and prediction, gaining expertise in building data structures that maximize utility is crucial. In this area, SQL plays a central role in facilitating database management.

Additionally, the R programming language is a popular choice for data science applications. Mastery in data handling forms an integral foundation for leveraging the full potential of AI, enabling you to skillfully and precisely navigate data transformation processes.

Understanding Computer Vision Principles

Computer vision involves training machines to perceptually understand visual stimuli. This empowers computers to derive meaningful insights from images, videos, and other visual inputs. These insights can then be used to trigger actions or generate recommendations.

Machines, with their processing speed, can outperform humans in analyzing thousands of images per minute. Like other AI learning modes, computer vision depends on large datasets to recognize fine distinctions and identify specific visual patterns. This skill is enhanced by algorithmic models within machine learning, allowing computers to independently comprehend the complexities of visual data.

Automated Code Generation

Automated programming involves a specialized form of computing where code is generated for other programs based on predefined specifications. A prominent example is **AlphaCode by DeepMind**, which demonstrated the ability to write code. In one case, AlphaCode faced coding competition challenges, such as transforming a random string of letters into another string with the same letters under specific constraints. AlphaCode approached the task by generating a wide array of potential solutions, running the code, evaluating the output, and analyzing each solution to identify the optimal one.

Learning Data Processing

Data processing is a fundamental pillar of learning AI from scratch—so crucial that it constitutes a standalone discipline. Today, big data is deeply embedded in nearly all aspects of modern life. Almost all organizations have embraced data-driven decision-making as an essential part of their strategy. This transformative power is realized through machine learning technology, which relies on skillful management of large datasets.

In AI learning, **data preprocessing** emerges as a vital task. It involves converting raw data into a structured format while ensuring its integrity. The quality of data depends on several critical attributes, including:

- **Completeness**
- **Timeliness**
- **Security**
- **Accuracy**
- **Consistency**

In the preprocessing phase, data is meticulously cleaned by removing errors, incomplete entries, or redundant information. This step integrates various data sources into a unified dataset. Finally, the data undergoes **reduction** and **transformation** to make it ready for use.

Building Machine Learning Solutions

The role of a machine learning engineer involves building AI systems capable of automating predictive models based on machine learning principles. These engineers use large datasets to conceptualize and nurture algorithms, enabling them to learn from outcomes and subsequently improve future task execution, achieving high accuracy in results.

Machine Learning

Machine learning is a key branch of artificial intelligence, where computers can autonomously enhance their processes with minimal human intervention. Remarkably, machine learning programs can decode complex and subtle patterns that often surpass human understanding.

This skill is gained through datasets and pattern recognition methods. The field includes two main categories: supervised and unsupervised learning, thoroughly discussed in the article on types of machine learning algorithms.

In supervised learning, data can be gathered or generated from previous machine learning outcomes. The computer has a training dataset with labeled data points, allowing it to recognize underlying patterns. In contrast, unsupervised learning involves algorithms attempting to uncover the inherent structural composition of data without relying on predefined training datasets.

Mastering Machine Learning

Starting the machine learning journey requires focused research in AI, needing a solid understanding of prerequisites and overarching AI theory. Beyond these fundamentals, here's a comprehensive roadmap to specialized machine learning learning:

1. **Learn Python**: As the foundational language in machine learning, Python serves as the gateway to this field.
2. **Master data science tools**: Equip yourself with essential tools like Jupyter and Anaconda, which enable seamless data manipulation, visualization, and analysis.
3. **Core data analysis tools**: Learn key tools like Pandas, NumPy, and Matplotlib. These allow you to effectively manipulate data.
4. **Harness Scikit-Learn**: Use the powerful Python library Scikit-Learn to discover patterns in your datasets, enabling insights and predictions.
5. **Master Deep Learning**: Unlock the potential of deep learning by mastering the construction of neural networks. Understanding deep learning complexities opens the door to advanced AI applications.
6. **Work on personal projects**: Deepen your learning by engaging in hands-on projects. This

practical experience reinforces your understanding and nurtures problem-solving skills.

Through this holistic approach, you will skillfully navigate machine learning and harness its power for decoding patterns, making predictions, and creating innovative solutions.

How is Machine Learning Related to Learning AI from Scratch?

Machine learning is a branch of AI. It's one method of implementing AI principles, enabling computers to learn without explicit programming.

Data Science Career

Data science has a symbiotic relationship with machine learning engineering, yet they are distinct fields. Data science is a comprehensive domain focused on deriving meaningful insights from data. In this broader landscape, machine learning serves as a powerful tool for working with data.

Data science involves using scientific methods, processes, algorithms, and systems to extract meaning and insights from unstructured data, recommended for complementing AI learning from scratch.

Role of a Data Scientist

Data scientists use machine learning and deep learning models to craft solutions tailored to business challenges. Unlike machine learning engineers, data scientists more often use existing machine learning tools for data processing but can design custom programs when needed.

After identifying business problems suitable for machine learning interventions, a data scientist formulates algorithms and models to address and solve these challenges.

Data Science Learning Path

Similar to mastering machine learning, exploring data science requires full understanding of AI prerequisites and core concepts. As a branch of AI, they share many foundational principles. The data science learning path includes:

″ Working on projects using available datasets: Enhance your expertise by working on projects that leverage existing datasets. Practical experience increases your skill and talent.

" Mastering data cleaning: A vital aspect of your data science journey is mastering the art of data cleaning.

Through these coordinated efforts, you gain solid knowledge in data science and boost your skills.

Relationship Between Data Science and AI

Data science and AI share a symbiotic relationship, where data scientists use AI technologies in their roles, leading to significant overlap between data science, machine learning, and AI. The key distinction lies in how these fields converge: data science uses AI and ML as tools for extracting insights.

Here, data science's pivotal role extends to human interpretation of results from machine learning to derive insights and meaningful conclusions. This complex interaction underscores the cohesive synergy between data science and the broader AI domain.

Data Engineer

Distinguishing between a data scientist and a data engineer can be challenging, especially when reviewing job listings. Notably, data scientists often take on data engineering responsibilities. Still, it's crucial to recognize these roles as essentially distinct. Data engineering embodies the art of visualizing data, transforming raw data into a functional and accessible format. Data engineers consolidate diverse data sources into a unified source ready for in-depth analysis.

Data Engineering Learning Path

In the journey of learning AI from scratch, understanding data engineering tasks is also essential. Mastery in data engineering requires skills in various areas including:

1. **Algorithms and Data Structures**: Mastery of algorithms and data structures enhances your ability to optimize data management processes.
2. **Distributed Systems**: A deep understanding of distributed systems strengthens your data handling across networks.
3. **Data Storage**: Learning the complexities of data collection and storage is foundational.
4. **ETL Tools**: Get familiar with ETL tools like Xplenty or Hevo, essential for data transformation.

5. **Familiarity with ML**: Understanding core ML concepts enriches your toolkit and enhances comprehensive understanding.
6. **Programming Languages**: Skills in languages like Python and Julia are crucial for implementing data-driven solutions.
7. **Database Systems Expertise**: Strengthen your data handling capabilities by mastering database systems, especially SQL.

Working on Suitable AI Projects

Another step in learning AI from scratch is engaging in practical projects. Navigating AI project sets requires a strategic approach. With AI's global applications, you have many options. Start with projects aligned with your interests and community needs.

″ Work on basic and simple projects: Some classic projects are consistently recommended for beginners and offer valuable foundational skills.

″ Interest-aligned projects: Choose projects that naturally align AI applications with your personal interests.

Highly recommended projects for learning AI from scratch include:

″ Stock price prediction
″ Face recognition
″ Human activity recognition
″ Sales price prediction
″ Fake news detection
″ Language translation

Using AI Tools

In the realm of learning AI from scratch, many tools are available. Below are the most essential ones:

″ **Scikit-Learn**: A standout in the ML library landscape, it's a valuable tool for supervised and unsupervised learning. Its versatility makes it ideal for beginners.

″ **PyTorch**: Known for strengths in areas like natural language processing and computer vision, it's widely applied in programs.

″ **TensorFlow**: With adaptability across various ML tasks, TensorFlow excels especially in training and inferring deep neural networks, adding extra power to your AI toolkit.

AI Internships

After completing courses and building a strong portfolio, starting an AI internship is a crucial step in completing your learning path. Internships significantly enhance your job-seeking efforts. A standout feature of AI internships is their ability to address real-world challenges.

AI Courses

The most common approach to learning AI from scratch is through training courses. You can choose structured training based on your preference and interest. Numerous online platforms offer AI and ML skills training. For example, platforms like Udemy and Coursera in English, and Maktabkhooneh in Persian, perform very well.

Is Practical Work Necessary for Learning AI?

Learning AI from scratch involves advanced concepts that may present challenges depending on your existing knowledge. Choosing a well-structured program simplifies facing these challenges. In general, learning AI requires both practical effort and theoretical understanding.

How Long Does It Take to Learn AI?

The time to learn AI from scratch and build a career path depends on your existing knowledge and learning journey. For beginners, understanding AI basics might take about six months. In contrast, exploring complex areas like data science might require pursuing an advanced degree over several years.

Can AI Be Learned Without Coding Skills?

Although certain platforms offer no-code AI solutions, mastering AI requires programming and coding skills. The foundation of AI learning lies in programming, and proficiency requires designing and implementing problem-solving algorithms.

Why Learn AI?

Gaining AI knowledge is a highly attractive and practical skill for addressing some of humanity's most vital challenges, such as diseases, environmental pollution, and climate change. Moreover, this field is rapidly growing economically. Learning AI equips individuals for a fulfilling and dynamic career path with numerous job opportunities.

Role of an AI Engineer

Tasks and responsibilities of an AI engineer may vary depending on their specific sector. Generally, AI engineers build AI systems and applications aimed at enhancing decision-making and improving performance metrics.

The role of an AI engineer is multifaceted and complex, requiring skills in the following areas:
" Achieving objectives through skillful use of AI models
" Innovating solutions through a mix of logical reasoning, probability analysis, and ML techniques
" Monitoring and directing development initiatives via comprehensive analysis of complex systems
" Gaining deep understanding and effectively implementing best practices in speech recognition, data processing, data mining, and robotics.

Learning AI from Scratch

You may ask yourself how to start AI or where to begin. Learning AI from the ground up requires going through several stages, summarized in 8 steps:

1. Learning AI fundamentals and prerequisites
2. Understanding theoretical AI concepts

3. Developing data processing skills
4. Creating and participating in AI projects
5. Getting familiar with AI tools
6. Attending AI-related courses
7. Doing internships in AI
8. Getting hired and starting to work in AI
   Starting AI from scratch comes with its own challenges, which every learner must face. Advanced math and logic can ease entry into this field. Below, the AI learning roadmap is explored in more detail across these 8 steps.

Programming Skills

Gaining programming skills in AI-relevant languages is essential for building AI applications.
Notable options include:
″ Python – popular for its accessibility, simplicity, rich libraries, and abundant resources
″ Java – known for its user-friendly nature and cross-platform compatibility
″ R – built for managing large datasets
″ Lisp – the second oldest programming language used in AI
″ SQL – has a core role in database management
″ and more

Key data structures include:

″ Array

″ Linked list

″ Stack

″ Queue

″ Binary tree

″ Binary search tree

″ Hash

″ Matrix

Understanding these structures allows AI learners to effectively manipulate data and enhance their ability to create impactful, efficient AI applications.

Algorithm Fundamentals

Working in AI requires a deep understanding of computer science fundamentals. An algorithm acts as a systematic guide, outlining step-by-step procedures for computations. In machine learning, it is essential to design algorithms capable of independent learning. These algorithms use data mining and pattern recognition to offer recommendations.

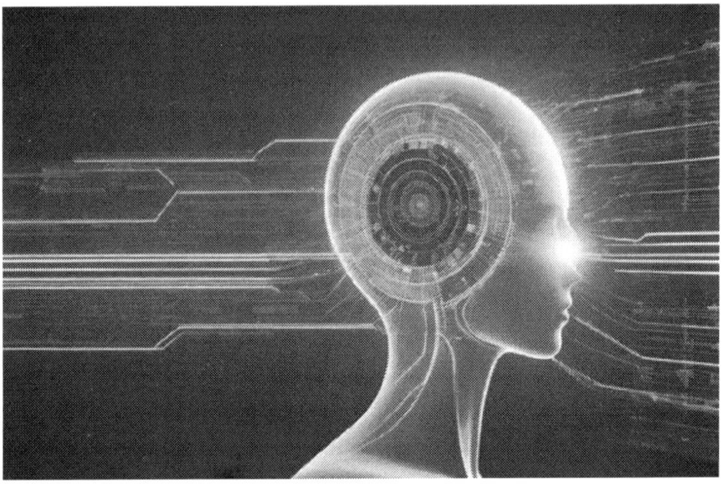

Machine Learning with Python

Problem Formulation

To pave the way for effective problem-solving, a structured process of problem formulation emerges—one that encompasses several critical components:

1. The initial state of the agent's environment
2. The set of permissible actions available to the agent
3. A transition model outlining the consequences of each action
4. A goal-testing mechanism that verifies whether the desired objective has been achieved
5. The cost associated with each traversed path

Mastery of these elements empowers learners to fully comprehend the intricacies of problem-solving in the field of artificial intelligence, laying a foundational cornerstone for the journey toward AI expertise.

Logical Inference

Given that machines inherently lack cognitive faculties, they rely on algorithmic planning to engage in reasoning processes. When programming AI to draw conclusions, the task involves training it to achieve goals through various modes of logical inference, including:

- **Deductive reasoning**: This form of reasoning leverages existing data to ensure the logical validity of premises. It entails applying general principles to specific instances.
- **Inductive reasoning**: In contrast to deduction, inductive reasoning extrapolates general conclusions from specific observations. In this case, a conclusion may be inaccurate even if all observations are factually correct.
- **Abductive reasoning**: This method aims to infer the most plausible explanation that aligns with the observed data. It resembles deduction but does not guarantee the truth of the conclusion.
- **Commonsense reasoning**: An informal approach that draws on experiential knowledge. It operates

based on heuristics and practical judgment, rather than formal logic.

- **Monotonic reasoning**: Yields conclusions that remain valid regardless of the addition of new data.
- **Non-monotonic reasoning**: Allows for conclusions to be revised in light of new information.

Acquiring proficiency in these reasoning paradigms equips AI practitioners with the tools to imbue artificial agents with inference capabilities—an essential step toward innovation and advancement across diverse AI applications.

Data Transformation

Learning artificial intelligence from the ground up necessitates a profound grasp of data manipulation. Given AI's dependence on datasets for learning and prediction, expertise in crafting data structures that optimize utility is paramount. Within this domain, the SQL programming language plays a pivotal role in facilitating database management. Furthermore, R has emerged as a favored language in data science applications.

Competence in data manipulation forms an indispensable foundation for unleashing AI's potential, empowering learners to navigate the complexities of data transformation with precision and finesse.

Training Sequence Models and Natural Language Processing (NLP)

One notable example involves AlphaCode, which faced a series of challenges akin to those found in competitive programming scenarios. For instance, one task required transforming a random sequence of characters into another string containing the same characters, albeit under constrained input conditions. AlphaCode approached the problem by generating a wide array of potential solutions, executing the produced code, evaluating the resulting outputs, and assessing each solution to identify the optimal choice.

Learning Data Processing

Data processing constitutes a fundamental pillar in the journey of learning AI from scratch—so vital, in fact, that it has evolved into a standalone discipline. In the modern era, big data has seamlessly integrated into nearly every facet of contemporary life. Nearly all enterprises have embraced data-driven decision-making as a core strategic component.

This transformative power is realized through machine learning technologies, which depend on the skillful handling of massive datasets. In foundational AI education, data preprocessing emerges as a pivotal endeavor, involving the transformation of raw data into an intelligible framework while preserving its integrity.

Key attributes defining data quality include:

- **Accuracy**
- **Consistency**
- **Completeness**
- **Timeliness**
- **Security**,

  among others.

Preprocessing involves rigorous steps to clean the data by removing inaccuracies, incomplete entries, or redundant information. This stage also integrates diverse data sources into a unified dataset. Ultimately, data is subjected to dimensionality reduction and transformation to render it suitable for analysis and learning.

Building Machine Learning Solutions

The role of a machine learning engineer involves developing AI systems capable of automating predictive models rooted in machine learning principles. These engineers leverage large-scale datasets to conceptualize and refine algorithms that learn from outcomes and subsequently enhance their performance in future tasks—thereby achieving high levels of predictive accuracy.

Machine Learning

Machine learning is a pivotal subfield of artificial intelligence that enables computers to autonomously refine their processes with minimal human intervention. Notably, machine learning systems can decipher complex and subtle patterns that often elude human cognition. This capability is achieved through data-driven learning and pattern recognition techniques.

The discipline is broadly categorized into two major paradigms: **supervised learning** and **unsupervised learning**, both of which are discussed in detail in the section on types of machine learning algorithms.

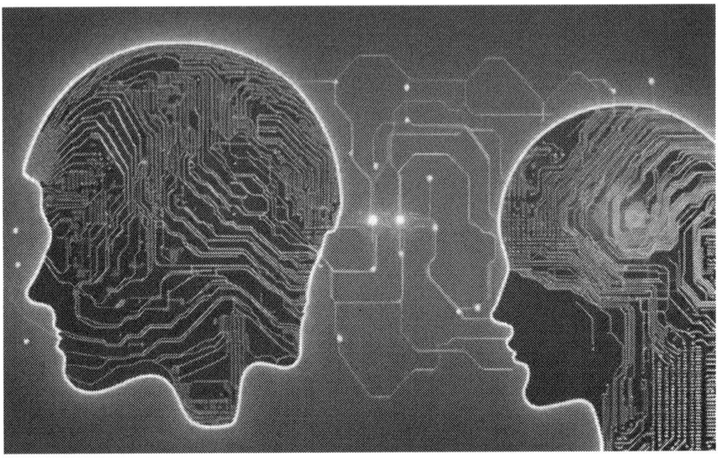

Supervised vs. Unsupervised Learning

In supervised learning, data can be collected or generated based on outcomes from previous machine learning processes. The computer is provided with a training dataset that contains labeled data points, enabling it to identify underlying patterns. In contrast, unsupervised learning centers around algorithms that attempt to uncover the intrinsic structural composition of the data without relying on predefined labeled datasets. This learning paradigm proves particularly effective in revealing previously undiscovered patterns embedded within the dataset.

Reinforcement Learning Training Pathway

- **Interest-Aligned Projects**: Choose projects that align AI applications with your personal interests to foster intrinsic motivation and practical relevance.
- **Beginner-Friendly Projects**: Engaging with foundational, entry-level projects is consistently recommended for newcomers. These projects deliver essential core skills and conceptual clarity.

Highly recommended project ideas for learning AI from the ground up include:

- **Fake News Detection**
- **Language Translation**
- **Stock Price Prediction**
- **Facial Recognition**
- **Human Activity Recognition**
- **Sales Price Forecasting**

Chapter 4:

Applications of Artificial Intelligence in Human Life

Introduction

Introduction

Artificial Intelligence (AI) is a technology endowed with the ability to simulate human-like thinking. It is a branch of computer science primarily focused on creating intelligent machines capable of performing tasks that traditionally require human intelligence. In essence, AI is the simulation of human cognitive processes within computational systems.

AI Technology

Artificial intelligence refers to a machine that is programmed to think in a manner similar to humans and capable of imitating human behavior. This definition applies to all machines that function in ways resembling the human mind—particularly in performing tasks such as problem-solving and learning.

AI is a broad subfield of computer science dedicated to building intelligent systems that can perform tasks typically requiring human cognition. As an interdisciplinary science, AI integrates various approaches; however, recent advancements in machine learning and deep learning have revolutionized nearly every domain of the tech industry.

The foundation of artificial intelligence lies in understanding and modeling the workings of human intelligence in such a way that a machine can replicate it to effectively carry out assigned tasks.

AI fundamentally revolves around three core objectives:

- **Learning**
- **Reasoning**
- **Perception**

How Does Artificial Intelligence Learn?

Today's AI systems become intelligent through **machine learning (ML)** and **deep learning (DL)**. These methods empower machines to learn from data and experiences, continuously improving their performance over time.

Each of these will be explored in the subsequent sections.

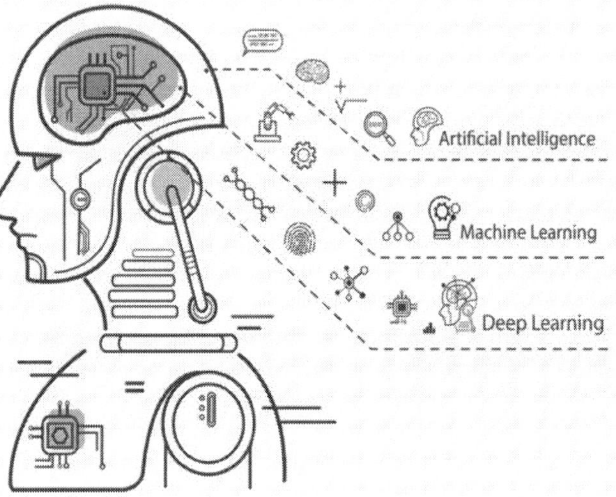

Machine Learning

Machine Learning (ML) is a subfield of artificial intelligence that enables systems to learn and improve automatically from experience, without being explicitly programmed. The central focus of machine learning is the development of computer programs that can access data and use it to autonomously enhance their performance.

In machine learning, the learning process begins with observations or data—such as examples, direct experience, or instructions—in order to identify patterns and make informed decisions based on those patterns. The fundamental objective of machine learning is to empower computers to learn automatically from data and adapt their behavior accordingly, without the need for continuous human intervention.

A wide array of machine learning algorithms exists, with hundreds of new ones emerging regularly. These algorithms are commonly categorized based on their **learning style**—such as **supervised learning**, **unsupervised learning**, or **semi-supervised learning**—or based on their **form and functionality**, such as **classification**, **regression**, **decision trees**, **clustering**, and **deep learning**.

Regardless of the categorization, most machine learning algorithms operate in relation to three key domains:

- **Representation**: A set of classifiers or a formal language comprehensible to the computer.
- **Evaluation**: Also known as the performance metric or scoring function.
- **Optimization**: A search strategy to identify the highest-performing classifier.

The ultimate aim of machine learning algorithms is to **accurately interpret data** and to **generalize learned knowledge** beyond the training instances.

Deep Learning

Deep Learning is a subset of machine learning and artificial intelligence that mimics the way the human brain processes and learns specific topics. It plays a critical role in data science, incorporating elements of statistics and predictive modeling. Deep learning significantly aids data scientists in collecting, analyzing, and interpreting vast volumes of data by automating and accelerating analytical processes.

Essentially, deep learning is an advanced form of machine learning that operates on **higher levels of abstraction**, enabling AI systems to recognize complex patterns and understand intricate aspects of the real world. At its simplest, deep learning can be understood as an approach that automates predictive analytics.

To comprehend how deep learning functions, one must understand **neural networks**. Deep learning models are composed of **multi-layered neural networks**, also referred to as deep neural networks. These models contain multiple hidden layers, and as data progresses through each layer, the system builds increasingly sophisticated and accurate representations of the input, leading to higher performance in complex tasks.

Levels of Artificial Intelligence

Artificial intelligence systems are typically classified into three distinct levels based on their ability to perceive and respond to the external world:

1. **Narrow AI (ANI – Artificial Narrow Intelligence):** Refers to AI systems that are designed and trained to perform specific tasks. These systems excel in their designated domains but lack general cognitive capabilities. Examples include facial recognition, language translation, and recommendation systems.
2. **General AI (AGI – Artificial General Intelligence):** Envisions machines with cognitive abilities comparable to that of a human being. AGI systems would be capable of performing any intellectual task that a human can do, including reasoning, problem-solving, and learning across domains.
3. **Superintelligent AI (ASI – Artificial Superintelligence):**
   A hypothetical future state in which AI surpasses human intelligence across all fields, including creativity, general wisdom, and social intelligence. ASI represents the pinnacle of AI development and raises profound ethical, philosophical, and existential considerations

Levels of Artificial Intelligence

Artificial Intelligence (AI) systems are classified into three distinct levels based on their cognitive capabilities and response mechanisms to external stimuli:

1) Artificial Narrow Intelligence (ANI)

Artificial Narrow Intelligence, also referred to as **Weak AI**, represents the earliest and most prevalent form of AI in use today. ANI systems are designed to perform specific tasks—often with performance levels that surpass human capabilities in those tasks. For example, computer programs capable of playing complex games such as chess, making smart business decisions, converting speech to text, or performing facial recognition in large crowds all fall under the category of narrow AI.

These systems are highly specialized and operate within pre-defined parameters. They do not possess general intelligence or awareness, and their capabilities are limited to their programmed domain.

2) Artificial General Intelligence (AGI)

Artificial General Intelligence refers to a hypothetical machine that possesses the ability to understand, learn, and apply knowledge across a wide range of tasks—similar to human cognitive ability. Unlike narrow AI, AGI would be capable of reasoning, problem-solving, and adapting to novel situations in the same way a human does.

Although AGI does not yet exist, it is often envisioned in science fiction narratives and theoretical discussions. The realization of AGI could fundamentally change the workforce, potentially replacing human involvement in many areas. While its emergence presents numerous opportunities to solve complex societal challenges, it also raises significant ethical and practical concerns. Potential applications of AGI range from smart personal assistants and autonomous vehicles to medical diagnosis systems capable of interpreting user intent and emotional context.

3) Artificial Superintelligence (ASI)

Artificial Superintelligence refers to an AI system that surpasses human intelligence in all respects—logic, creativity, emotional intelligence, and general wisdom. ASI is purely theoretical at this stage, and no existing society has achieved it. The timeline, feasibility, and implications of achieving ASI remain uncertain and are the subject of ongoing debate among scientists and technologists.

In theory, a superintelligent AI would be capable of solving problems beyond human comprehension. However, its emergence poses existential questions: Will it be a threat or an ally to humanity? For an AI to reach the ASI stage, it would need to pass the **Turing Test** and demonstrate a level of consciousness and understanding equivalent to or exceeding that of a mature human—something no AI has yet accomplished.

Applications of Artificial Intelligence

AI technologies have found extensive application across various domains. One of the most impactful sectors is **healthcare**, where AI is transforming diagnosis, treatment, drug discovery, and patient management.

Applications of AI in Medicine and Healthcare

AI is revolutionizing medical science through its ability to detect genetic patterns, assist in complex surgeries, and interpret medical imagery. It enhances diagnostic accuracy and operational efficiency in healthcare environments.

Key applications include:

1) Accurate Diagnosis and Reduction of Medical Errors

Incomplete access to a patient's medical history is a significant cause of medical errors. AI systems can analyze large datasets rapidly, helping predict and diagnose diseases with higher accuracy and fewer errors, especially in critical care.

2) AI-Powered Drug Discovery

Pharmaceutical companies are increasingly leveraging AI to reduce the cost and time associated with drug research and development. On average, clinical testing of a single drug costs approximately $2.6 billion, and only 10% make it to market. AI can optimize this process by predicting molecular interactions and identifying potential compounds for clinical trials.

3) Streamlining the Treatment Process

Innovative AI technologies improve the patient experience by enabling hospitals to manage and process vast amounts of data more efficiently. AI facilitates personalized treatment and enhances decision-making by medical staff.

4) Medical Data Management

The healthcare industry is being reshaped by **big data** and AI. Often, valuable insights are buried within millions of data points, making it difficult to extract actionable knowledge. AI enables healthcare professionals to detect patterns and anomalies swiftly, helping accelerate diagnostics, treatment planning, and drug development.

5) AI-Assisted Robotic Surgery

AI-powered robots are being used in various surgical procedures—from minimally invasive methods to open-heart surgeries. These robots, equipped with cameras and surgical tools, enhance surgical precision beyond human capabilities. Surgeons control robotic arms via computer interfaces, gaining 3D visualizations and magnified images of the surgical site. This innovation has introduced a new era in surgical care.

AI Trends in Healthcare During the COVID-19 Pandemic

The **COVID-19 pandemic** accelerated AI adoption across the global healthcare sector. Organizations turned to AI to manage increased demand, assist with vaccine research, and transition to **telehealth** solutions. Leading tech companies such as **NVIDIA** and **Alibaba** employed AI to detect COVID-19 symptoms in CT scans. Nursing homes and elder care centers began implementing AI-based passive monitoring systems to reduce healthcare workers' exposure risk.

As a result, investment in AI health tech companies surged. In the **third quarter of 2020 alone**, over **$2 billion** was invested in this sector, marking a record high (Sehat, 1399).

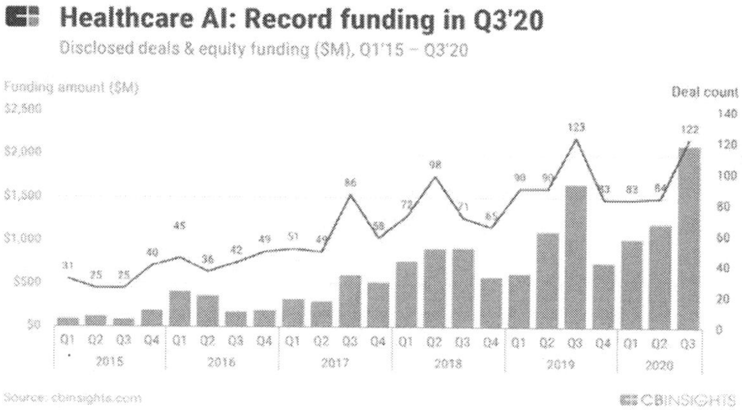

With the maturation of the AI industry, companies are attracting increasingly higher levels of investment in each funding round. Since March 2020, eleven health AI companies have collectively raised close to **$100 million**, primarily aimed at leveraging AI for **drug research and development**. Some of the patterns that emerged during the COVID-19 pandemic are expected to exert **long-lasting influence** on the healthcare industry.

Hospitals and the Shift Toward AI-Based Robotic Process Automation (RPA) for Revenue Cycle Management

Despite the relatively **slow adoption** of robotic process automation (RPA) technologies in healthcare compared to other industries, **demand for these solutions surged** during the pandemic.

Studies have revealed that **administrative costs** in U.S. hospitals are among the **highest globally**, accounting for nearly **25%** of total healthcare expenditure. Recent analyses estimate this to be approximately **$2,500 per patient**.

Hospital administrative staff, in addition to their routine responsibilities, are often engaged in **revenue-related tasks** such as:

- Verifying patients' insurance eligibility,
- Assigning accurate medical billing codes,
- Filing claims with insurers,
- Tracking and resolving unpaid patient invoices.

Robotic Process Automation (RPA), a general term for automating repetitive tasks—including **employee onboarding** and **digitizing documents**—has benefited significantly from advancements in **computer vision** and **natural language processing (NLP)**. Although initial enthusiasm around RPA's impact on revenue cycles has diminished somewhat, many hospitals have only recently begun to recognize its operational benefits.

One reason for the slow uptake may be that **most RPA vendors** offer **generalized solutions** across multiple industries, rather than developing platforms that are **specifically tailored** to the technical and regulatory challenges unique to the healthcare sector.

Case Study: Olive—AI-Driven RPA in Healthcare

Olive, a company originally launched in 2012 as a **patient intake portal**, was quick to identify the opportunity in **AI-based RPA for hospitals**. By focusing on healthcare-specific process automation, Olive positioned itself as a **pioneer** in the space.

Currently, the company serves **over 600 healthcare providers** and has raised **more than $230 million** in investment to date.

Overview · Transactions · Signals · IP · Competition · Network

Funding 7 Fundings / $233.3M

Date	Round	Amount	Investors
9/17/2020	Series F	$106M	Ascension Ventures, General Catalyst, and 3 more
3/31/2020	Series E	$51M	Ascension Ventures, General Catalyst, and 2 more
7/30/2018	Series D	$32.8M	Ascension Ventures, and Oak HC/FT Partners
12/13/2017	Debt	$8.5M	Undisclosed Investors
4/6/2016	Series C	$15M	Khosla Ventures, Silicon Valley Bank, and 3 more
4/14/2015	Series B	$15M	Khosla Ventures, and Drive Capital
8/7/2013	Series A	$5M	Drive Capital

Transformation in the Software Service Model with Building AlphaSites

Olive has gone beyond the traditional Software-as-a-Service (SaaS) model by building **AlphaSites** in hospitals and deploying engineering and project management staff on-site to carry out implementation operations.

Alpha Health, a startup, raised $20 million in June 2020 from Andreessen Horowitz and other investors to develop a similar revenue cycle management service.

Automation of Charge Capture Process with AI

Another part of the revenue cycle simplified by AI is **charge capture**, the process where physicians

convert patient visits and diagnoses into medical codes that are submitted as bills to insurers.
Assistant companies like Suki and Augmedix use voice technology and Natural Language Processing (NLP) to transcribe doctor-patient interactions and automatically update Electronic Health Records (EHR). Their digital medical assistants can also suggest relevant medical codes based on the conceptual information obtained from these interactions.

Reducing IT Costs in Hospitals; Increasing Demand for Automation

While many hospitals aim to reduce IT costs due to the economic impacts of COVID-19, the demand for services from companies like Olive—which raised over $150 million in funding during two investment rounds amid the pandemic—indicates hospitals are likely interested in cutting long-term costs and automating parts of their financial management processes.

Faster, Cheaper, better: The Next Generation of MRI and CT Imaging

AI in imaging not only reduces costs but also shortens the patient's time at imaging centers, thus lowering exposure to radiation and heavy metals during the imaging process.

One leading AI application in healthcare is **computer vision** in medical imaging to detect anomalies in scans and assist in disease diagnosis.

Since 2014, with the entrance of major tech companies and numerous startups, the market has flooded with AI-powered diagnostic imaging products. Many quickly adapted their products to detect COVID-19 signs in lung CT scans.

The impact of AI-assisted diagnostic methods on healthcare costs will be increasingly scrutinized in the coming months.

Case Study: Ezra – Replacing Biopsy with MRI in Prostate Cancer Diagnosis

Ezra AI aims to replace the expensive and invasive prostate biopsy with MRI, which is a cheaper alternative.

Ezra claims its AI software, recently FDA 510(k) approved, not only improves diagnostic accuracy over traditional biopsy but also automates the radiologist's workflow, making MRI a cost-effective and competitive method.

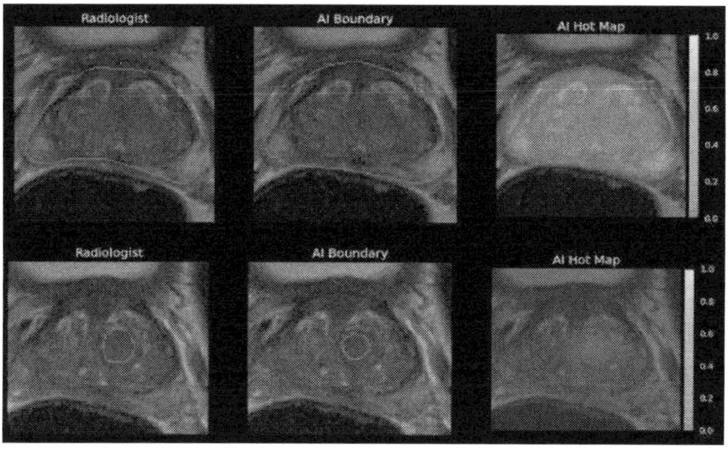

Transformation in the Software Service Model with Building Alpha Sites

Olive has gone beyond the traditional Software-as-a-Service (SaaS) model by building **Alpha Sites** in hospitals and deploying engineering and project management staff on-site to carry out implementation operations.

Alpha Health, a startup, raised $20 million in June 2020 from Andreessen Horowitz and other investors to develop a similar revenue cycle management service.

Automation of Charge Capture Process with AI

Another part of the revenue cycle simplified by AI is **charge capture**, the process where physicians convert patient visits and diagnoses into medical codes that are submitted as bills to insurers.

Assistant companies like Suki and Augmedix use voice technology and Natural Language Processing (NLP) to transcribe doctor-patient interactions and automatically update Electronic Health Records (EHR). Their digital medical assistants can also suggest relevant medical codes based on the conceptual information obtained from these interactions.

Reducing IT Costs in Hospitals; Increasing Demand for Automation

While many hospitals aim to reduce IT costs due to the economic impacts of COVID-19, the demand for services from companies like Olive—which raised over $150 million in funding during two investment rounds amid the pandemic—indicates hospitals are likely interested in cutting long-term costs and automating parts of their financial management processes.

Faster, Cheaper, better: The Next Generation of MRI and CT Imaging

AI in imaging not only reduces costs but also shortens the patient's time at imaging centers, thus lowering exposure to radiation and heavy metals during the imaging process.

One leading AI application in healthcare is **computer vision** in medical imaging to detect anomalies in scans and assist in disease diagnosis.

Since 2014, with the entrance of major tech companies and numerous startups, the market has flooded with AI-powered diagnostic imaging products. Many quickly adapted their products to detect COVID-19 signs in lung CT scans.

The impact of AI-assisted diagnostic methods on healthcare costs will be increasingly scrutinized in the coming months.

Case Study: Ezra – Replacing Biopsy with MRI in Prostate Cancer Diagnosis

Ezra AI aims to replace the expensive and invasive prostate biopsy with MRI, which is a cheaper alternative.

Ezra claims its AI software, recently FDA 510(k) approved, not only improves diagnostic accuracy over traditional biopsy but also automates the radiologist's workflow, making MRI a cost-effective and competitive method.

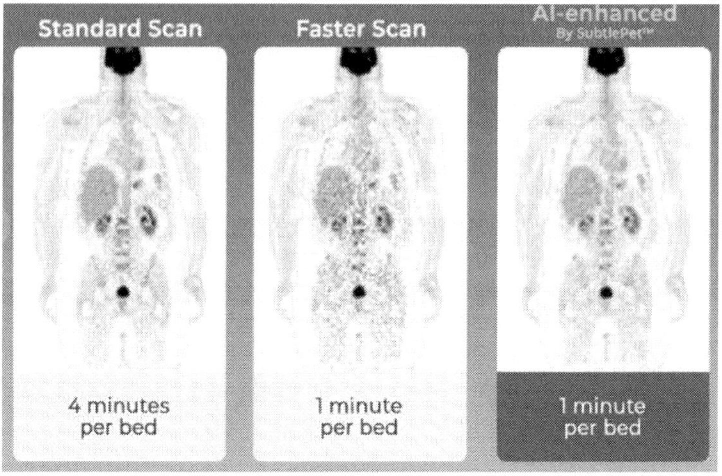

Subtle Company: Enhancing Faster Scans and Higher-Quality MRI and PET Images Using AI

Subtle is working on improving image quality in MRI and PET scans through artificial intelligence to achieve faster scanning and better images. In August 2020, the company received a $6.1 million grant from the National Institutes of Health (NIH). The purpose of this grant is to develop new AI software capable of reducing the dose of gadolinium—a heavy metal used to help evaluate tumors—administered to patients during MRI imaging.

According to reports, gadolinium can have long-term toxic effects in the body, and its use in MRI scans is limited in conditions such as chronic kidney disease. AI-based image enhancement, as one of the diagnostic AI methods, significantly reduces the costs associated with radiology scans and also improves patient health and accessibility.

Instant Blood Tests and Rapid Home Testing: AI Eliminates the Need for Labs in Some Tests!

Computer vision technology turns smartphones into powerful diagnostic tools that reduce the need for expert interpretation in some tests.

Gauss Surgical, an AI company, entered the healthcare market with a platform that monitors blood loss in operating rooms. During COVID-19, the company expanded its technology to become a diagnostic tool for users.

Gauss collaborated with biotechnology company Cellex to produce a rapid COVID-19 test kit. Users of Cellex's home test kit receive training on how to properly use a nasal swab, then scan the test with their smartphone via the Gauss app. Image processing is done through an artificial neural network, and the test result is reported within seconds.

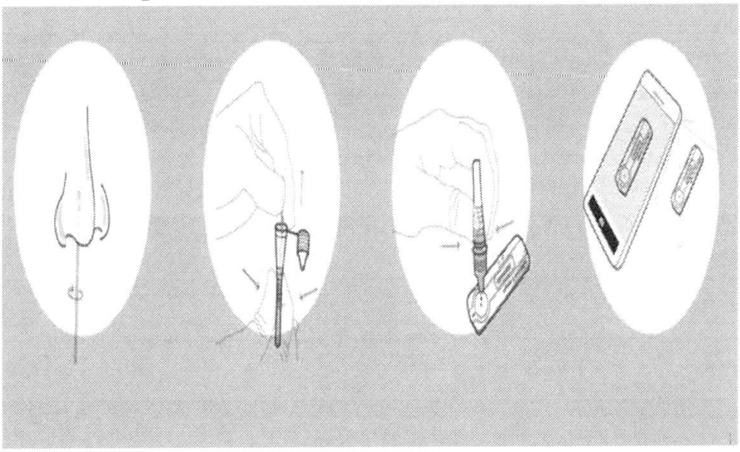

Gauss Company Claims That the New Gauss-Cellex Test Enables Non-Experts to Interpret At-Home Antigen Tests Using AI

Gauss claims that its new Gauss-Cellex test, which makes antigen detection possible at home, leverages its AI technology to allow non-specialist users to interpret results using an iPhone or Android smartphone after performing the test.

Although molecular PCR tests for COVID-19 are more accurate, their results can sometimes take up to a week to be delivered. Due to the need to accelerate review and final approval processes during the pandemic, the FDA granted emergency approval to companies like Cellex. Cellex's product is an antibody test that can be completed in labs within just 15 minutes.

Nowadays, companies like Gauss, relying on computer vision technology, have further increased diagnostic speed and made these methods available on patients' smartphones.

Healthy.io: A Simple Urine Test and Analysis Method as Easy as Taking a Selfie

Healthy.io designed a method for urine testing and analysis that is as simple as taking a selfie. Its first product, Dip.io, uses conventional dipstick urine tests to monitor different degrees of urinary tract infections. The test strip is scanned with a smartphone camera and analyzed by computer vision algorithms.

The company later expanded its apps to include prenatal tests and home testing for chronic kidney diseases. Computer vision technology not only benefits user tests but also enables rapid point-of-care testing (POCT) outside traditional labs. For example, certain blood tests can be performed without a lab using this technology.

Sight Diagnostics, a company that raised $71 million during the pandemic, developed a complete blood count (CBC) analyzer that delivers test results within minutes. This technology is awaiting FDA approval for point-of-care use (outside traditional labs) in the US.

Remote Pathology (Telepathology): AI and Digital Slides Become a New Norm for Laboratories

The shortage of specialists and social distancing measures accelerated the adoption of digital pathology and AI. Although AI adoption in pathology lagged behind radiology, after the COVID-19 pandemic and labs' embrace of digital technologies for better response, pathology gradually began integrating AI.

The usual workflow involves taking a tissue or biological sample from the patient, staining it, and sending it to a pathologist. The pathologist examines the sample under a microscope, and if a definitive diagnosis cannot be made, the sample is packaged and sent to another pathologist for review.

A post from the Google AI blog highlights the complexity and diagnostic challenges of pathology slides.

Examining pathology slides is extremely complex, requiring years of training and practice. Still, there are significant discrepancies in diagnoses for the same sample among different pathologists, which can lead to misdiagnosis. For example, in some breast and prostate cancers, diagnoses agree in only 48% of cases.

Digital Pathology and AI

In digital pathology, high-resolution images of stained samples are captured using imaging devices. Pathologists can review these images on computers remotely rather than using microscopes. This technology also enables pathologists to collaborate with other specialists via cloud-based software and use AI to analyze images and assist in diagnosis.

In 2017, Google published research on using deep learning to identify tumors in microscopic samples

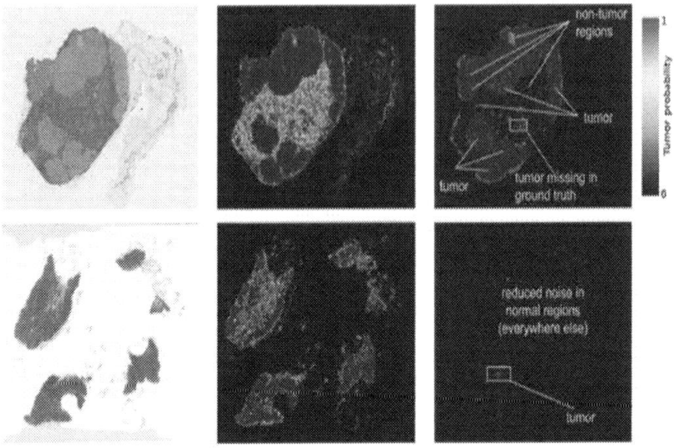

In the same year, the FDA approved the first whole slide imaging system (IntelliSite Pathology Solution) designed by Philips.

This device was capable of capturing and storing high-resolution images of tissue samples. This technology sparked increased interest in digital pathology.

LabCorp, one of the largest laboratory networks in the United States, announced last year in a press conference that its investment in AI for pathology is a long-term investment without immediate tangible effects. However, the current health crisis and the need for remote work have accelerated this trend.

The ability to implement remote work for employees has never been considered a problem for laboratories,

but the COVID-19 pandemic and increased workload and stress pushed us to seriously consider a collaborative workflow suitable for remote work.
Paige AI, an AI company active in cancer detection in New York, raised $5 million in funding in April 2020 through Goldman Sachs, and an additional $20 million in July. The company cites increased demand for its products during the pandemic as a key factor. The shift toward digital pathology is a global phenomenon.
In the UK, Ibex Medical Analytics, active in AI-based pathology, has partnered with London Digital Pathology, a supplier in this field. The CEO of LDPath predicted that after the pandemic ends, due to a significant increase in testing requests, pathology workloads will rise sharply. Partnerships with other companies help them better manage this situation. The UK has long faced a shortage of pathology specialists, which can delay cancer diagnosis by weeks.
CorePlus Laboratory, specializing in prostate cancer diagnosis in Puerto Rico, announced in September 2020 that after partnering with Ibex, it switched its diagnostic method from traditional microscope-based pathology to AI-based pathology.

Recently, Philips partnered with Singapore General Hospital to smarten workflow in the pathology department, aiming to save nearly 12,000 hours annually.

Overall, the shortage of pathologists worldwide is a common problem, and many predict that after the pandemic, there will be a sharp rise in laboratory test demand. Stakeholders who have been reluctant to digitalize or smarten their operations will now be compelled to use telepathology and AI technologies.

Artificial Intelligence: Innovation and Efficiency in Early Drug Discovery

AI has played a role in various stages of new drug discovery—from understanding virus structure to identifying effective compounds—significantly reducing the time to develop drugs from years to months.

Introducing a new drug to market typically takes nearly a decade or more from initial research to distribution. However, with governments pushing vaccine development for COVID-19, pharmaceutical companies have accelerated this timeline severalfold. With the pandemic onset, startups, universities, and big pharma have used AI to better understand the structure of this novel virus, discover new and effective treatment compounds, find previously FDA-approved drugs for repurposing, and even design stable molecular drugs.

Researchers at the University of Texas at Austin and the NIH used software called cryoSPARC to study the SARS-CoV-2 structure. Using 2D images from cryo-electron microscopy (a technique capturing molecular structures), they successfully designed a 3D virus model. cryoSPARC, developed by Structura Biotechnology, uses artificial neural networks to solve particle picking—identifying and isolating protein structures in microscopic images.

Google also employs AI in drug discovery. Last year, DeepMind, a Google subsidiary, designed the AlphaFold algorithm that helps identify protein folding, one of the most complex genomic challenges, enabling more precise 3D protein structure determination. During the pandemic, DeepMind used AlphaFold to model the COVID-19-related protein and made it publicly available.

Recursion Pharma, an AI-based biotech company, released a large dataset on SARS-CoV-2. In September 2020, they raised $239 million in Series D funding with investors like Leaps by Bayer, Lux Capital, and Data Collective. Recursion used AI by infecting healthy cells with SARS-CoV-2 in a controlled environment, then analyzing microscopic images with deep learning to identify physical changes caused by infection.

Atomwise, an AI platform for small-molecule drug R&D, has collaborated with Columbia University, Jazan University, Dana-Farber Cancer Institute, and others to produce broad-spectrum coronavirus drugs.

Cyclica uses AI for new drug discovery in infectious diseases, including COVID-19, partnering with Mannin Research.

French company Iktos collaborates with SRI International to use its AI platform to design new molecules for influenza, SARS-CoV-2, and other viral diseases.

AI will accelerate future drug discovery. Despite significant progress in identifying drugs against the pandemic (WHO announced over four vaccine candidates entered clinical trials), not all advancements are solely due to AI—advanced computational modeling remains a critical part of drug discovery and production.

From Specialized Care Centers to Quarantine Wards: A Leap in Passive AI-Based Monitoring

Tools that can passively and contactlessly measure physical parameters of the human body reduce the risk of virus exposure for healthcare workers. Beyond the current crisis, these technologies can form the backbone for health service delivery. The advantage of passive monitoring is that unlike wearable devices, patients do not need to wear anything continuously.

Additionally, automated data collection of vital signs from hospitalized patients limits contact between healthcare staff and COVID-19 patients, reducing virus transmission risk.

A research team at MIT designed a device called Emerald, installed in hospital rooms, that emits signals analyzed via machine learning after reflection. Emerald can differentiate patients in the same room by their movement patterns and can sense patients through walls, detecting subtle movements like chest rises for respiratory pattern analysis.

Currently, this technology is used by Heritage Assisted Living in Boston to monitor COVID-19 patients.

Federated Learning: Collaboration Between Hospitals and Pharma Companies to Improve AI Use

AI-based federated learning, which preserves data security, started with Google's text prediction feature on Android keyboards and is now expanding in pharma, hospitals, and other sectors.

Federated learning allows companies to enhance AI algorithms while protecting user data privacy, making it well-suited for sensitive fields like healthcare. Google was the first to use this approach for predicting text input on Android keyboards.

Basic AI Algorithms

The most important AI algorithms are called basic algorithms because anyone interested in learning AI must become familiar with them.

Basic Artificial Intelligence Algorithms

Artificial Intelligence (AI) algorithms are a set of methods and techniques that enable AI systems to perform complex tasks typically requiring human intelligence. These algorithms encompass decision-making, learning from data, simulating human reasoning, machine learning, and solving intricate problems. The primary goal of AI algorithms is to allow systems to automatically learn and improve from data and experience without explicit programming for each specific task.

AI Search Algorithms

Search algorithms in AI are powerful tools for solving complex problems where finding the appropriate solution among many options is essential. These algorithms employ different approaches to identify the best path or solution within the problem space. Generally, search algorithms are categorized into three main types: informed search, which uses additional information about the problem to guide the search more effectively; uninformed search, which relies solely on the problem's structure without prior knowledge; and local search, which directly navigates the state space focusing on incremental improvement of the solution. Below is a more detailed discussion of these algorithms and their applications.

Informed Search Algorithms

Informed search algorithms utilize extra information about the problem to guide the search process more efficiently. This information usually comes in the form of an evaluation or heuristic function estimating the cost to reach the goal from a given state. By leveraging this heuristic, the algorithm prioritizes options more likely to lead to the goal, thus reducing the number of states explored and reaching a solution faster.

Informed search algorithms are considered fundamental AI algorithms widely applied in various problems. One common tool is the heuristic function, which estimates the cost from the current state to the goal and guides the search towards the optimal path. For example, in finding the shortest path between two points on a map, the straight-line distance can serve as a heuristic.

Examples of informed search algorithms include:

- **A***: This algorithm combines the cost so far (g(n)) and the estimated remaining cost (h(n)) to select the best path. Due to its optimality and completeness, A* is widely used.

- **Greedy Best-First Search**: This method focuses only on h(n) (the estimated cost to the goal) and selects states closest to the goal according to the heuristic. Although fast, it may not always find the optimal solution because it ignores the cost already incurred.

Informed search algorithms are extensively used in complex problems such as routing, computer games, and combinatorial problems, with the main advantage being reduced time and resource consumption.

Uninformed Search Algorithms

Uninformed or blind search algorithms do not utilize any additional information about the problem structure or the distance to the goal. They rely only on the initial state, goal state, and transition rules to explore the search space. Compared to informed algorithms, uninformed searches are less efficient because they may explore many unnecessary states. Nevertheless, uninformed search remains a foundational AI approach useful when no heuristic information is available.

Key characteristics of uninformed search algorithms include:

- No heuristic or pre-existing information for estimating closeness to the goal.

- Systematic exploration of all possible paths and states.
- Optimality and completeness depend on the implementation and problem characteristics.

Common uninformed search algorithms:

- **Depth-First Search (DFS)**: Explores as deeply as possible before backtracking. Memory-efficient but may get stuck in infinite loops or find non-optimal solutions.
- **Breadth-First Search (BFS)**: Explores all nodes at one depth level before moving deeper. Guarantees optimal solutions when costs are uniform but requires significant memory.
- **Depth-Limited Search**: A variant of DFS with a fixed depth limit to prevent infinite loops but may miss solutions beyond the limit.
- **Bidirectional Search**: Simultaneously searches from the start and goal nodes, reducing the number of explored nodes but requires knowledge of the goal state.
- **Uniform-Cost Search**: Selects nodes with the lowest path cost from the start, guaranteeing optimal paths, unlike BFS which only considers depth.

Uninformed searches are useful in basic problem-solving when heuristics are unavailable, but for more complex problems, informed methods are preferred.

Local Search Algorithms

Local search algorithms focus on a small portion of the search space rather than the entire space, aiming to iteratively improve the current solution. Starting from an initial state, these algorithms explore neighboring states and move towards optimal or near-optimal solutions. This approach is especially useful in large search spaces where exhaustive search is impractical. Local search algorithms are fundamental in AI and are widely applied in optimization and NP-hard problems.

Characteristics of local search:

- Focus on the current state and its neighbors.
- Low memory usage, storing only a few states.
- No guarantee of finding a global optimum; may get trapped in local optima.

Types of local search algorithms:

- **Hill Climbing**: Moves to the best neighbor state at each step. Simple and fast but prone to getting stuck in local optima or plateaus.

- **Simulated Annealing**: Inspired by the physical annealing process; occasionally accepts worse states with a decreasing probability to escape local optima.
- **Beam Search**: Examines multiple states simultaneously but limits the number of states retained at each step, balancing completeness and efficiency.
- **Genetic Algorithms**: Based on biological evolution concepts, evolving populations of states using selection, crossover, and mutation to approach optimal solutions.

Supervised Learning Algorithms

Supervised learning algorithms, a major category in machine learning, train models using labeled data where the input-output mapping is known. Their goal is to predict output values based on inputs. They are divided into regression (predicting continuous values) and classification (predicting categorical labels). These algorithms form a core part of AI and have broad applications.

Key supervised algorithms include:

- **Logistic Regression**: Used for binary classification, modeling the probability that an input belongs to a class using a sigmoid function. It can be extended for multiclass problems. Known for simplicity and interpretability but less effective for complex nonlinear relationships.

- **Linear Regression**: Predicts continuous values assuming a linear relationship between inputs and output, minimizing mean squared error. Simple and widely used but limited for nonlinear data.
- **K-Nearest Neighbors (KNN)**: A non-parametric algorithm that classifies a new sample based on the majority class among its k closest neighbors. Simple but less efficient in high-dimensional spaces.
- **Support Vector Machines (SVM)**: Finds an optimal hyperplane separating classes with maximum margin. Uses kernel functions to handle nonlinear data. Offers high accuracy and resistance to overfitting but computationally intensive on large datasets.
- **Decision Trees**: Models decisions with tree structures, splitting data by features to maximize information gain or reduce impurity. Easy to interpret but prone to overfitting without pruning.

- **Random Forests**: An ensemble of decision trees trained on random data subsets and feature subsets to improve accuracy and reduce overfitting. Robust but computationally more expensive.

Unsupervised Learning Algorithms

Unsupervised learning algorithms identify hidden patterns in data without labeled outputs. They are used for clustering, dimensionality reduction, anomaly detection, and data visualization. Common algorithms include k-means clustering, hierarchical clustering, principal component analysis (PCA), and autoencoders.

And other similar tasks are utilized. Unlike supervised learning, where models are trained using labeled data, unsupervised learning algorithms aim to discover the inherent structure or patterns within raw data.

K-Means Clustering

K-Means clustering is one of the most popular and widely used clustering algorithms in machine learning, applied to divide data into similar groups or clusters. The objective of this algorithm is to partition the data into *k* clusters such that similar data points belong to the same cluster and the clusters are distinct from each other. The K-Means algorithm operates based on the mean of the data points within each cluster and seeks to minimize the sum of the squared distances between each data point and its cluster center.

Typically, K-Means proceeds in several steps: initially, *k* cluster centers are chosen randomly. Then, each data point is assigned to the nearest cluster center. Subsequently, the cluster centers are updated as the mean of the data points belonging to each cluster. This process continues until the cluster centers stabilize or change minimally.

One of the challenges of this algorithm is selecting the appropriate *k* value, as *k* determines the number of clusters and must be chosen carefully to ensure meaningful data partitioning. Methods such as the Elbow method assist in choosing the proper *k*. As one of the foundational AI algorithms, K-Means is generally suitable for large datasets but can yield variable and suboptimal results due to its sensitivity to the initial cluster center selection.

Hierarchical Clustering

Hierarchical clustering is a clustering method that organizes data into a tree-like structure called a dendrogram. It can be performed in two main ways: bottom-up (agglomerative) and top-down (divisive). In the bottom-up approach, each data point initially forms its own cluster, and similar clusters are gradually merged until all data points belong to a single cluster. In the top-down approach, all data points start within one cluster and are progressively divided into smaller clusters.

Hierarchical clustering algorithms use various similarity or distance metrics to measure the closeness between clusters. Common metrics include Euclidean distance, Manhattan distance, and correlation distance.

At each step, the closest clusters are merged, gradually forming the cluster tree. This algorithm is a foundational AI method often suited for data with hierarchical structure, where clusters form progressively at multiple scales. Advantages include not requiring a predetermined number of clusters (k), but drawbacks include high computational complexity for large datasets.

DBSCAN Clustering

DBSCAN (Density-Based Spatial Clustering of Applications with Noise) is a density-based clustering algorithm effective at identifying clusters in complex data with noise. Unlike other clustering algorithms like K-Means, which require a fixed number of clusters, DBSCAN automatically determines the number of clusters and can detect noise points (outliers).

DBSCAN operates based on two main parameters: ε (Epsilon) and MinPts. The parameter ε defines the radius within which points must lie to be considered neighbors, while MinPts specifies the minimum number of points required to form a cluster.

The clustering process begins by examining each data point. If a point has enough neighboring points within distance ε, it is considered a core point and forms a cluster, with neighboring points added accordingly. Points not belonging to any cluster are identified as noise. DBSCAN is a foundational AI algorithm with advantages such as identifying clusters of arbitrary shapes and robustness to noise. However, it may struggle with very dense or sparse data, as the choice of ε and MinPts parameters is sensitive.

t-SNE Dimensionality Reduction

t-SNE (t-Distributed Stochastic Neighbor Embedding) is a dimensionality reduction technique designed specifically for visualizing high-dimensional data. This algorithm improves the analysis of complex and large datasets by mapping them into a lower-dimensional space while preserving local similarities between data points. In other words, t-SNE analyzes data so that distances and relationships in the high-dimensional space are optimally represented in two- or three-dimensional space.

t-SNE is commonly used to visualize high-dimensional data such as images, text, and features extracted from machine learning models. It first computes similarities between points in the original space and then maps them to a low-dimensional space such that points close in the original space remain close in the reduced space.

A key feature of t-SNE is its ability to identify clusters and complex structures in data that are not easily observable by other dimensionality reduction methods. Recognized as a foundational AI algorithm, t-SNE is highly useful for data visualization, especially with high-dimensional data. However, it is primarily a visualization tool rather than a method for direct learning or prediction. Also, selecting appropriate parameters like learning rate and number of dimensions significantly affects the results.

Reinforcement Learning Algorithms

Reinforcement Learning (RL) algorithms are a category of machine learning methods where an agent interacts with an environment to learn optimal decision-making policies that maximize cumulative reward over time. The agent receives feedback from the environment, usually in the form of rewards or penalties, and aims to learn a policy that leads to maximum long-term reward. In other words, in each state, the agent chooses an action to increase cumulative future rewards.

Q-Learning is a reinforcement learning algorithm that helps an agent learn the best strategy (policy) for various tasks through environmental interaction. It employs a model-free, unsupervised learning approach to determine the best action in each state. Q-Learning uses a Q-table, which stores the value of each state-action pair.

In this algorithm, the agent is in a state and must select an action, receiving a reward and transitioning to a new state. The goal is to learn Q-values so that, in each state, the action with the highest Q-value is chosen, maximizing long-term rewards. Due to its model-free nature, Q-Learning is widely applied in reinforcement learning problems such as games, robotics, and autonomous systems.

Reinforcement Learning in Python

The DQN (Deep Q-Network) algorithm is a reinforcement learning technique that uses deep neural networks as function approximators to estimate the Q-function, enabling AI to learn optimal policies in complex environments. Instead of a Q-table, a neural network predicts Q-values for all states and actions. As a foundational AI algorithm, DQN is efficient for large state spaces, as neural networks generalize effectively to unseen states. DQN uses experiences collected from environment interactions to update the network continuously.

A key feature of DQN is Experience Replay, where past interaction experiences are stored and randomly sampled for training the neural network, preventing data correlations and stabilizing learning. Additionally, DQN employs a Target Network updated periodically to avoid oscillations in network updates. These techniques make DQN effective for learning complex behaviors in real-world environments like video games or robotics.

REINFORCE is another foundational AI algorithm, a policy-gradient-based reinforcement learning method that improves stochastic policies in complex environments. Unlike value-based methods like Q-Learning, REINFORCE directly updates the policy. The policy is modeled as a probability distribution over actions in each state, updated using reward feedback from the environment.

Each time an action is selected under the current policy, cumulative rewards from that action guide parameter updates. Specifically, the policy gradient is adjusted proportionally to the received rewards, gradually improving the policy. Although simpler than other reinforcement methods, REINFORCE can have high reward variance, leading to slow learning, often requiring variance reduction techniques for effective training.

Machine Learning Algorithms

Various foundational AI algorithms have been reviewed, each with diverse and valuable applications in specific fields. From search algorithms to machine learning and reinforcement learning methods, these

techniques enable AI systems to solve complex problems, learn from data, and make optimal decisions.
With rapid advances, AI algorithms are becoming powerful tools across industries including healthcare, autonomous vehicles, commerce, and data analytics. Familiarity with these algorithms is essential not only for researchers and IT engineers but also for anyone seeking to better understand and leverage AI's capabilities in daily life.

Artificial Intelligence Can Prescribe Different Versions

Artificial intelligence enables the provision of learning models tailored to the individual capabilities and backgrounds of learners. Undoubtedly, people's learning models differ from one another; instructors can use AI to pay attention to these differences and offer personalized learning models to students.

Instructors take various actions based on feedback they receive from the classroom; however, a teacher in a class of 60 students cannot provide multiple versions of course content personalized to individual students' characteristics. Moreover, the limitation of instructors in the classroom is not only about prescribing a common version. They cannot focus on each student individually, but with the help of AI, they can prescribe diverse versions and monitor the progress of each student. The educational journey is like a trip, and each person requires a separate plan.

We Should Not Expect Education to Remain the Same with the Entry of AI

There are many pros and cons to consider regarding technology. Some believe AI reduces creativity because students use AI tools to solve problems and do not put effort into solving them themselves. Does AI really reduce creativity? I believe AI helps nurture creativity. When technology enters education, we should not expect education to continue as it currently is. Learning models will undoubtedly change. For example, nowadays we ask students to memorize some educational content, but by leveraging AI, we can guide them toward reasoning and problem analysis. Students' creativity grows better with AI tools available to them.

Paying attention to students' creativity is important and sensitive. With the advent of generative AI, especially ChatGPT, the fear of losing students' creativity has become a concern. Advanced countries have considered the issue of declining creativity with AI and concluded that students with AI have access to vast resources and can delegate problem-solving to AI. However, if students use AI merely to complete their assignments without engaging in the learning process, the purpose of the assignments is lost.

The Way Questions Are Asked Must Change

Advanced countries have concluded through research that the way questions are posed must change. As university instructors, we should shift from superficial questions to analytical questions and guide students toward reasoning and analysis. This change in question structure helps develop students' reasoning and creativity. As long as answers can be found with a simple internet search, we cannot expect students to answer difficult questions in industrial and professional contexts.

Can AI Be Applied to All Academic Disciplines?

Although AI technology can be used in all academic fields, the degree of its application varies. Where visualized models are available, AI use will be more intense. For example, AI can help simulate cellular or molecular structures in biology or chemistry. AI can provide a 3D perspective on many issues and is highly useful in fields like mechanical engineering. Conversely, its role may be less significant in pure mathematics.

Generative AI, such as ChatGPT, can assist in teaching subjects like literature or English language studies. Today, the idea of delegating foreign language education to generative AI has been proposed. Still, AI does not have an equal impact across all disciplines currently; its impact is broader in some fields and more limited in pure sciences, though this may change in the future.

From a Hardware Perspective, We Lag Behind Advanced Countries

To reduce our gap with leading countries in AI, we must focus on three areas: hardware, software, and intellectual resources.

We are not far behind in software and intellectual resources compared to advanced countries, but there is a significant gap in hardware. University equipment is very different from that in leading countries. Currently, even basic classroom tools like projectors have issues. This problem also exists in schools. We should not forget that many schools face fundamental problems like heating systems and still struggle with issues such as old heaters catching fire. Under such circumstances, it might be premature to talk about widespread AI adoption in schools.

Many Countries Have Developed Roadmaps for AI Implementation

Many countries have seriously planned for AI development. The first step is for governance to believe in AI and new technologies and to use local experts to develop roadmaps for AI application. Budgets for new technologies should be allocated; sometimes budgets are set but without proper frameworks, leading to wasted funds. Moreover, suitable cultural adaptation for AI adoption must be carried out to see beneficial results in society.

Continuous and Regular Training for Instructors

Today, we must train students for jobs that do not yet exist. The same applies to AI use in education. When some instructors were younger, many current technologies did not exist. Naturally, there is a gap between what we learned years ago and what we need to apply now. To bridge this gap, continuous and regular training for instructors is necessary. We should not easily lose experienced instructors; instead, a team approach can be used. One instructor can lead teaching while a team of teaching assistants, often graduate students, help those less familiar with new technologies. Students are ahead in AI adoption; when generative AI emerged, students quickly learned to use it, while instructors, depending on their roles, should keep up with current technologies. Still, infrastructure weaknesses cause difficulties, like asking students to bring laptops but facing internet and electricity issues.

Defining Business Intelligence for Classrooms

Many companies work in business intelligence but have not entered education, causing a technology gap in this sector. Whether willingly or not, AI will hold an important place in education. Traditional teaching models will undergo major changes. If managers, students, and instructors do not adapt to new technologies, they will be left behind. Technology will continue advancing, and the roles of instructors and students will change; AI can handle course content delivery, while instructors act as coaches helping students navigate their learning paths.

Organizational Budgeting in the Era of Generative AI

Many organizations and companies have tried for over a decade to apply traditional AI and automation. However, since the launch of OpenAI's ChatGPT at the end of 2022, there has been a major shift in organizational AI priorities toward generative AI, enhancing traditional AI and creating new functionalities. After initial excitement, enterprise customers are realizing that implementing AI requires strategic and financial commitment. As one manager noted, "Expanding AI is hard and requires new skills, processes, and ways of working. This will be a transformative challenge for most organizations."

McKinsey Research

Recent McKinsey research shows that 67% of surveyed organizations expect to allocate over a third of their technology budgets to AI and generative AI within three years. Overall technology budgets are projected to grow 4-6% CAGR over five years, with spending shifts due to new value pools and competitors.

Service Development

Generative AI has expanded service offerings. For example, hyperscalers provide integrated environments to build, train, customize, and deploy large language models (LLMs). Hardware companies offer services to develop personalized LLMs and microservices for faster AI software development.

Budget Areas

New competitors are one aspect of disruption. Main categories of IT service budgets are:

- Traditional outsourced services: declining 8-10% due to AI-driven automation addressing legacy IT challenges.
- Insourced IT services: steady budgets despite increased workloads from low-code/no-code platforms and AI tools.
- Hybrid cloud services (public/private): likely growth in specialized AI workloads, with possible reductions elsewhere.

New Opportunities

Budget increases have led to new AI opportunities:

- Outsourced AI services: expected double-digit growth, driven by cost concerns and lack of in-house AI expertise pushing companies toward external help. Spending focuses on AI infrastructure, horizontal problem-solving (e.g., programming copilots), and vertical industry solutions (e.g., biotech clinical trials, B2C telecom).

- Outsourced digital services: increased demand for cloud, legacy
- modernization, data, and analytics, growing 8-12% as AI integrates into digital programs.
- Enterprise software: significant growth due to AI-powered new software generation addressing traditional IT challenges.
- AI infrastructure problem-solving methods: fast-growing new expense category for foundational models and similar costs.
- Public cloud and infrastructure as a service: AI drives cloud adoption and migration with specialized cloud AI providers.
- Computing hardware like GPUs: rising investment as companies use AI chips and cloud providers invest in advanced hardware.

The Future of AI: Will AI Replace Human Jobs?

Replacing today's workforce with AI systems is a likely future scenario. Although general AI won't replace all jobs, the nature of work will change through automation, with speed and extent of transformation varying. AI cannot work alone; while many routine data jobs can be automated, employees in other roles will use generative AI tools to boost productivity. Experts differ on AI's rate of surpassing human abilities. Fully autonomous vehicles aren't yet reality, but the autonomous transport industry alone may replace over 500,000 jobs in the U.S. Development and implementation costs are barriers to full AI workforce replacement. Positively, AI also creates new jobs, some yet unknown. Thus, as AI advances, its positive effects on job creation must be considered.

Persian References

- "Recent Advances in Pediatric Dentistry" – Tehran Dentistry Journal
- Ai Housh: The Importance of Artificial Intelligence in Higher Education
- Arab, Yazdi, and Mahmoudi (2023); Investigating the Dimensions of Academic Engagement of Accounting Students in University E-Learning Programs (Scientific Article, Ministry of Science); Empirical Accounting Research, Year 11, Fall 2022, Issue 45, pp. 201-220
- Ghaffari et al. (2023); LSTM Modeling and Optimization of Rice Seedling Growth Model (Oryza sativa L.) in a Smart Controlled Environment; Journal of Artificial Intelligence and Data Mining, Volume 11, Issue 4 (Autumn 2023)
- Ghanad et al. (2023); Application of Text Mining Techniques in Thematic Flow Analysis of Articles Published in Iranian Accounting Journals; Scientific Article, Ministry of Science: Financial Accounting and Auditing Research, Year 15, Summer 2023, Issue 2 (No. 58), pp. 1-38
- Jafari et al. (2023); Artificial Intelligence and New Technologies in Educational Systems:

Opportunities and Challenges; Article related to: Volume 4, Issue 4 (Winter 2023)

- Kazemi (2018); Providing an Intelligent Model for Selecting Suitable Suppliers Based on Combination of Data Envelopment Analysis and SVM; Iranian Journal of Management Studies, Volume 11, Issue 2 (Spring 2018)
- Moradi et al. (2024); Measuring and Anomaly Detection of Complexity in Accounting Records (Scientific Article, Ministry of Science); Accounting and Auditing Reviews, Volume 31, Fall 2024, Issue 3, pp. 598-634
- Saadat (2008); Camera Placement in Designing Industrial Photogrammetry Networks Using Multi-objective Evolutionary Optimization; Journal of Faculty of Engineering, University of Tehran, Volume 42, Issue 3 (Mapping No. 113), Summer
- Scientific Articles in Medical Databases
- Shabrandi et al. (2023); Rapid Prediction of COVID-19 Infection Using Household Data and Machine Learning Classification Algorithms: A Case Study of Iran; Journal of Artificial Intelligence and Data Mining, Volume 11, Issue 4 (Autumn 2023)

- Sohrabi (2012); Operations Research and Artificial Intelligence: Suitable Tools for Solving Combinatorial Optimization Problems; Management Knowledge, Issue 57, 2012
- Tehran Pediatric Dentistry Website
- Zakariania et al. (2024); Reasonable and Conventional Algorithms and Reinforcement of the Theory of Attributability of Civil Liability of Artificial Intelligence; Journal of Contract Law and New Technologies, Volume 5, Issue 1 (Spring and Summer 2024)
- Zakriaei et al. (2023); A New Hybrid Method Based on Machine Learning Techniques for Cancer Risk Detection; Journal of Artificial Intelligence and Data Mining, Volume 11, Issue 4 (Autumn 2023)

English References

- (2017). Do mandatory risk factor disclosures predict the level of future cash
- (2020). Tax avoidance, uncertainty,
- (raed) on providing guidance to instructors. arXiv preprint arXiv:1247,24424.

- Abernathy, J. L., Finley, A. R., Rapley, E.T., & Stekelberg, J. (2021). External
- academic research, and practice. Journal of Information, Communication and Ethics in Society.
- Accounting Review, 84(3), 969–999.
- Accounting Review, 88(3), 977-1005.
- activity in financial statements. NationalTax Journal, 57(3), 739–756.
- aggressive than non-family firms?.Journal of Financial Economics, 95(1),41-61.
- aggressiveness. Journal of Accounting Research, 50(3), 775-810.
- Allingham M. G., & Sandmo, A. (1972).Income tax evasion: A theoreticalanalysis. Journal of Public Economics,1(3-4), 323–338.
- American Academy of Pediatric Dentistry
- and control and corporate tax avoidance.Journal of Accounting and Economics,56(2-3), 228-250.
- and firm risk. Uncertainty and Firm Risk.
- and Learning Tools, 76, 188-.771
- Approach. 1426 4th International Conference on Wireless and Telematics (ICWT), 2-8.
- Arlinghaus, B. P. (1998). Goal setting and performance measures – by tax

- Artificial Intelligence Education. IEEE Access, 1, 224556-.175422
- Association, 40(2), 63-81
- auditor responses to tax risk. Journal ofAccounting, Auditing & Finance, 36(3),489-516.
- Austin, C. R., & Wilson, R. (2017). Anexamination of rcputational costs and taxavoidance: Evidence from ifrms with.valuable consumerbrands. The Journal of
- avoidance. The Accounting Review, 83(1),61-82.
- Bardertscher, B. A., Katz, S. P., & Rego,S. O. (2013). The separation of ownership
- BaturinElectrical Engineering. ‹O.I. ‹Lyfar ‹V.O. ‹Zahozhai ‹O.I. ‹& Ivanov ‹V.G. (1414). UNIFORM
- Bauer, A. M., & Klassen, K. J. (2014).Estimating downside tax risk: Explorationof unfavorable tax settlements. WorkingPaper.
- Becker, G. S. (1968). Crime andpunishment: An economic approach.Journal of Political Economy, 76(2), 169–217.
- Blouin, J. L., Krull, L. K., & Robinson, L.A. (2012). Is US multinational dividendrepatriation policy influenced by reportingincentives?. The Accounting Review,87(5), 1463–1491.

- Brown, J. L. (2011). The spread ofaggressive corporate tax reporting: Adetailed examination of corporate-ownedlife insurance shelter. The AccountingReview, 86(1), 23–57.
- Burkhard, M. (1411). STUDENT PERCEPTIONS OF AI-POWERED WRITING TOOLS:
- Cain, C.C., Buskey, C.D., & Washington, G.J. (1413). Artificial intelligence and conversational agent
- Campbell, J. L., Cecchini, M., Cianci, A.M., Ehinger, A. C., & Werner, E. M.
- Chan, C. K. Y., & Hu, W. (1413). Students' Voices on Generative AI: Perceptions, Benefits, and Challenges
- Chen, K. P., & Chu, C. C. (2005). Internal control versus external manipulation: A
- Chen, S., Chen, X., Cheng, Q., & Shevlin,T. (2010). Are family firms more tax
- Comput. Educ. Artif. Intell., 3, 244454.
- Contribute to Certificate Management of Students. TELKOMNIKA Indonesian Journal of
- corporate tax avoidance. Journal ofBanking & Finance, 72, 184-200.

- Cotton, D. R. E., Cotton, P. A., & Shipway, J. R. (1413). Chatting and cheating: Ensuring academic integrity
- De Simone, L. (2016). Does a commonset of accounting standards affect tax-motivated income shifting formultinational firms?. Journal ofAccounting & Economics, 61(1), 145–165.
- Dechow, P. M., Sloan, R. G., & Sweeney,A. P. (1995). Detecting earnings
- Desai, M. A., & Dharmapala, D. (2006).Corporate tax avoidance and high-
- Desai, M. A., Dyck, A., & Zingales, L(2007). Theft and taxes. Journal ofFinancial Economics, 84(3), 591-623.
- Developments, 1413 – Volume 1.
- Drake, K. D., Lusch, S. J., & Stekelberg,J. (2019). Does tax risk affect investor
- Dyreng, S. D., & Lindsey, B. P. (2009).Using financial accounting data to
- Dyreng, S. D., Hanlon, M., & Maydew, E.L. (2008). Long-run corporate tax
- Dyreng, S. D., Hanlon, M., & Maydew, E.L. (2019). When does tax avoidance resultin tax uncertainty?. The AccountingReview, 94(2), 179-203.

- Dyreng, S. D., Hanlon, M., Maydew, E.L., & Thornock, J. R. (2017). Changes incorporate effective tax rates over the past25 years. Journal of Financial Economics,124(3), 441-463.
- Dyreng, S. D., Hoopes, J. L., & Wilde, J.H. (2016). Public pressure and corporatetax behavior. Journal of AccountingResearch, 54(1), 147–186.
- Economics, 5(1), 119-149.the American Taxation Association, 39(1),67-93
- Education. 1413 International Conference on Computing, Electronics & Communications
- educational technology and a professional development program to improve it. Br. J. Educ. Technol.,
- Educators. International journal of artificial intelligence in education, 2–6. Advance online
- Engineering (iCCECE), 233-236.
- evolution – a cautionary tale of the benefits and pitfalls of advanced technology in education,
- examine the effect of foreign operationslocated in tax havens and other countries
- financial statement information. TheAccounting Review, 85(5), 1693–1720.
- firm risk?. Available at SSRN 2186564.Hutchens, M., Rego, S. O., & Williams,

- flows and stock returns? Evidence fromtax risk factor disclosures. Working
- Frank, M. M., Lynch, L. J., & Rego, S. O.(2009). Tax reporting aggressiveness andits relation to aggressive financialreporting. The Accounting Review, 84(2),467–496.
- Goodman, G. R. (2004). Internal controlsfor the tax department. Tax Notes, 103,579–588.
- Graham, J., Hanlon, M., Shevlin, T., &Shroff, N. (2014). Incentives for tax
- Guenther, D. A., Krull, L. K., &Williams, B. M. (2021). Identifyingdifferent types of tax avoidance:Implications for empirical research. TheJournal of the American TaxationAssociation, 43(1), 27-50.
- Guenther, D. A., Matsunaga, S. R., &Williams, B. M. (2017). Is tax avoidance
- Guenther, D. A., Wilson, R. J., & Wu, K.(2019). Tax uncertainty and incremental
- Guidelines for Responsible Implementation. International Journal of Research and Innovation in
- Hamdan, S.R., Kusdiyati, S., Khasanah, A.N., & Djamhoer, T.D. (1412). Early Detection of Children with

- Hanlon, M., Maydew, E. L., & Saavedra,D. (2017). The taxman cometh: Does taxuncertainty affect corporate cashholdings?. Review of Accounting Studies,
- https://axiomq.com/blog/7-emerging-technologies-that-will-reshape-education-in-1413/
- https://doi.org/24,2464.24743117,1413,1214246
- https://www.unesco.org/en/digital-education/artificial-intelligence
- Huang, H., Lobo, G., Wang, C., & Xie, H.(2016). Customer concentration and
- Hutchens, M., & Rego, S. O. (2015).Does greater tax risk lead to increased
- Improve Early Detection of Children with Special Needs.
- in Higher Education. arXiv preprint arXiv:1345,44114.
- in the era of ChatGPT. Innovations in Education & Teaching International, 2-21.
- Information Technologies, 16, 2442-.4842
- INTERACTION MODEL OF EDUCATIONAL PROCESS AGENTS IN THE UNIFIED
- International Conference on Cognition and Exploratory Learning in the Digital Age (CELDA)1141.

- International Conference on Computational Science and Computational Intelligence (CSCI), 841-
- Joo, S., Kim, J., & Kim, S. (1413). Establishment of data mining-based public education administrative
- Journal of Clinical Pediatric Dentistry
- Khasanah, A.N., Djamhoer, T.D., Kusdiyati, S., & Hamdan, S.R. (1414). Designing Teacher Training to
- Kizilcec R. F. (1413). To Advance AI Use in Education, Focus on Understanding
- Kulkarni, A. (1412). Towards understanding the impact of real-time ai-powered educational dashboards
- Labadze, L., Grigolia, M., & Machaidze, L. (1413). Role of AI chatbots in education: systematic literature
- Language Processing in K-21 Education. arXiv preprint arXiv:1324,42843.
- Learning with VR and AR Technologies. Futurity Education, 3(4), 15-227.
- Lisowsky, P. (2010). Seeking shelter:Empirically modeling tax shelters using
- Lisowsky, P., Robinson, L., & Schmidt,A. (2013). Do publicly disclosed tax

- Lo, C. K. (1413). What Isthe impact of ChatGPT on education? ARapid review of the Literature. Education
- MANAGEMENT SYSTEM OF A HIGHER EDUCATION INSTITUTION. Information Technologies
- management. The Accounting Review, 70,193–225.
- market?. European Accounting Review,28(4), 767-789.
- Markowitz, H. (1952). Portfolio selection.The Journal of Finance, 7(1), 77-91.
- Markowitz, H. (1959). Portfolio selection:Efficient diversification of investments.
- McGill, G. A., & Outslay, E. (2004). Lostin translation: Detecting tax shelter
- metaanalysis. British Journal of Educational Technology, 54(3).
- https://doi.org/24,2222/bjet.23334
- Mills, L. F., Nutter, S. E., & Schwab, C.M. (2013). The effect of political
- Minn, S. (1411). AI-assisted knowledge assessment techniques for adaptive learning environments.
- model of corporate income tax evasion.RAND Journal of Economics, 36(1), 151-164.

- Mollick, E. R., & Mollick, L. (1411, December 21). New modes of learning enabled by AI chatbots:
- Mon, B.F., Wasfi, A., Hayajneh, M., & Slim, A. (1413). A Study on Role of Artificial Intelligence in
- Mujtaba, D.F., & Mahapatra, N.R. (1414). Artificial Intelligence in Computerized Adaptive Testing. 1414
- Mulyana, E., Hakimi, R., & Hendrawan (1426). Bringing Automation to the Classroom: A ChatOpsBased
- Nazaretsky, T., Ariely, M., Cukurova, M., & Alexandron, G. (1411). Teachers' trust in AI-powered
- Neuman, S. S., Omer, T. C., & Schmidt,A. P. (2016). Assessing tax risk:
- New York: John Wiley & Sons.
- Nirmalyan, M., & Ks, S. (1414). The Adaptive Assessment - AI technique to help people evaluate their
- Observations from the past decade. TheJournal of the American Taxation
- of Artificial Intelligence in Education.
- on teacher conceptions of teaching Artificial Intelligence (AI) in K-21 schools. Education and

- on US multinational firms' tax rates.Journal of Accounting Research, 47(5),1283-1316.
- Paper.
- Perera, P., & Lankathilaka, M. (1413). AI in Higher Education: A Literature Review of ChatGPT and
- planning and avoidance: Evidence fromthe field. The Accounting Review, 89(3),991-1023.
- powered incentives. Journal of FinancialEconomics, 79(1), 145-179.
- Practitioner perspectives. Working Paper.
- professionals in fortune 500 companies.The Tax Executive, 50(6), 434–442.
- publication. https://doi.org/24,2447/s44513-413-44352-4
- Rego, S. O., & Wilson, R. J. (2012).Equity risk incentives and corporate tax
- related to firm risk?. The Accounting Review, 92(1), 115-136.
- reserves tell us about privately disclosedtax shelter activity?. Journal ofAccounting Research, 51(3), 583–629.
- review. International Journal of Educational Technology in Higher Education, 14.
- Saavedra, D. (2019). Is tax volatilitypriced by lenders in the syndicated loan

- Sciences, 23(4), 424. https://doi.org/24,3314/educsci23444424
- sensitivity and bargaining power on taxes:Evidence from federal contractors. The
- Shevchuk, I., Filippova, L., Krasnova, A., & Bazyl, O. (1413). Virtual Pedagogy: Scenarios for Future
- skills.
- Smart Learning Environments, 24. https://doi.org/24,2268/s44582-413-44137-x
- Social Science.
- Special Needs by Educators. International Journal of Pedagogy and Teacher Education.
- T Tian, X., & Boyer, K. E. (1413). A Review of Digital Learning Environments for Teaching Natural
- Tambuskar, S. (1411). Challenges and Benefits of 7 ways Artificial Intelligence in Education Sector. Review
- tax avoidance. The Accounting Review,94(2), 229-247.
- Teaching Machine Learning in K–21 Classroom: Pedagogical and Technological Trajectories for
- Tech services and generative AI: Plotting the necessary reinvention (2024). Anuj Kadyan, Himanshu Pandey, Noshir Kaka, Pallav Jain,

Senthil Muthiah, and Vikash Daga, with Ruchika Dasgupta, representing views from McKinsey's Technology, Media & Telecommunications Practice.

- Tedre, M., Toivonen, T., Kahila, J., Vartiainen, H., Valtonen, T., Jormanainen, I., & Pears, A. (1412).
- Three methods and assignments. SSRN. Retrieved from https://ssrn.com/abstract=4344763
- Tlili, A., Shehata, B., Adarkwah, M.A., Bozkurt, A., Hickey, D., Huang, R., & Agyemang, B. (1413).
- TOWARDS INDIVIDUALIZED TEACHING STRATEGIES. Proceeedings of the 21th
- Tzoneva, I. (1413). Benefits and challenges in using AI-powered educational tools. Education and New
- valuation of tax avoidance?. Journal ofAccounting, Auditing & Finance, 34(1),151-176.
- What if the devil is my guardian angel: ChatGPT as a case study of using chatbots in education.
- Wilde, J. H., & Wilson, R. J. (2018).Perspectives on corporate tax planning:
- Wilson, R. J. (2009). An examination ofcorporate tax shelter participants. The

- work automation system and student activity analysis. Journal of Autonomous Intelligence.
- Wu, R., & Yu, Z. (1413). Do AI chatbots improve students learning outcomes? Evidence from a
- Yau, K.W., Chai, C.S., Chiu, T.K., Meng, H.M., King, I., & Yam, Y. (1411). A phenomenographic approach
- Zaman, B.U. (1413). Transforming Education Through AI, Benefits, Risks, and Ethical Considerations.
- Zimmerman, J. L. (1983). Taxes and firm size. Journal of Accounting and.

Made in United States
Orlando, FL
05 November 2026

90229895R00103